CW00825934

all that beauty

LETTER MACHINE EDITIONS   SEATTLE, WA

all that beauty

Fred Moten

Published by Letter Machine Editions
Seattle, Washington
© 2019 by Fred Moten
All Rights Reserved
Book design by HR Hegnauer
Cover art by Wu Tsang, "Be Seen Thru"
Printed in the USA
Cataloging-in-Publication Data is on file at the Library of Congress
ISBN: 978-1-7327721-1-3
lettermachine.org
Distributed to the trade by Small Press Distribution (spdbooks.org)

Versions of some of what is gathered here have appeared in the journals *Hambone*, *Harper's*, *Kalfou*, *Neck*, *Poem-a-Day*, *The A-Line*, *The New Inquiry*, *The Volta*; as an index for Lauren Berlant & Kathleen Stewart, *The Hundreds*, published by Duke University Press in 2019; in the catalogues *Among Others: Blackness at MoMA*, published by the Museum of Modern Art in 2019, *Harry Dodge: Works of Love*, published by the Art Gallery, Aidekman Art Center, Tufts University in 2019; *Radio Imagination: Artists and Writers in the Archive of Octavia E. Butler*, published by Clockshop in 2018, *Zoe Leonard: Survey*, published by Prestel in 2018; *Soo Kim: A Week Inside Two Days*, published by MW Books in 2018; and *Artes Mundi 7*, published by Artes Mundi Press Limited in 2016; on a postcard published by Infinite Editions in 2018; in a chapbook called *from Day*, published by Belladonna in 2017; and in another book called *Who Touched Me?* by Wu Tsang and Fred Moten, published by If I Can't Dance, I Don't Want To Be Part Of Your Revolution in 2016. Thanks, finally, to Jericho Brown for sounding out and shedding light o'n'em.

for Brent Hayes Edwards

aprefatory note

About my interests: I don't know if I have any, unless the morbid desire to own a sixteen-millimeter camera and make experimental movies can be so classified.

Notes of a Native Son

When I was very young, and was dealing with my buddies in those wine- and urine-stained hallways, something in me wondered, *What will happen to all that beauty?* For black people, though I am aware that some of us, black and white, do not know it yet, are very beautiful. And when I sat at Elijah's table and watched the baby, the women, and the men, and we talked about God's—or Allah's—vengeance, I wondered, when that vengeance was achieved, *What will happen to all that beauty then?*

The Fire Next Time

My father said, during all the years I lived with him, that I was the ugliest boy he had ever seen, and I had absolutely no reason to doubt him. But it was not my father's hatred of *my* frog-eyes which hurt me, this hatred proving, in time, to be rather more resounding than real: I have my mother's eyes. When my father called me ugly, he was not attacking me so much as he was attacking my mother. (No doubt, he was also attacking my real, and unknown, father.) And I loved my mother. I knew that she loved me, and I sensed that she was paying an enormous price for me. I was a boy, and so I didn't really too much care that my father thought me hideous. (So I said to myself — this judgment, nevertheless, was to have a decidedly terrifying effect on my life.) But I thought that he must have been stricken blind (or was as mysteriously wicked as white people, a paralyzing thought) if he was unable to see that my mother was absolutely beyond any question the most beautiful woman in the world.

So, here, now, was Bette Davis, on that Saturday afternoon, in close-up, over a champagne glass, pop-eyes popping. I had caught my father not in a lie, but in an infirmity. For, here, before me, after all, was a *movie star: white*: and if she was white and a movie star, she was *rich*: and she was *ugly*.

I felt exactly the same way I felt, just before this moment, or just after, when I was in the street, playing, and I saw an old, very black, and very drunk woman stumbling up the sidewalk, and I ran upstairs to make my mother come to the window and see what I had found: You see? You see? She's uglier than you, Mama! She's uglier than me! Out of bewilderment, out of loyalty to my mother, probably, and also because I sensed something menacing and unhealthy (for me, certainly) in the face on the screen, I gave Davis' skin the dead-white greenish cast of something crawling from under a rock, but I was held, just the same, by the tense intelligence of the forehead, the disaster of the lips: and when she moved, she moved just like a nigger. Eventually, from a hospital bed, she murders someone, and [Spencer] Tracy takes the weight, to Sing Sing. In his arms, Davis cries and cries, and the movie ends. "What's going to happen to her now?" I asked Bill Miller. "We don't know," said Bill, conveying to me, nevertheless, that she would probably never get over it, that people pay for what they do.

The Devil Finds Work

The truth to which criticism has access fades to blur and we're sorry for our reckless scrutiny. But the study that soils transparency, in the rightful belief that it reveals an opacity that's always there, need offer no apology to James Baldwin since it's he who teaches us to look so closely that we see all dark through what we see. Criticism is supposed to let you see (through) that. Criticism is poetry, in this regard and, in this regard, Baldwin is more + less than either critic or poet or both. He makes us let us look for ourselves, and through ourselves, till we're beside ourselves. To be beside ourselves with holy looking is to practice Baldwin's selflessness, which is only his to give away in demanding that we see through him, too, in pursuit of impure, eccentric fugue rather than the chaste satisfaction that's said to live in one-on-one relation. Fugitive in small groups, dispossession flays the pair's impossible monogamy and folds to nothing, where there are no things. Such movement intimates black indecision, which is given in the setting of the scene, which incompletes, unsettles and upsets the scene. It's inappropriate and inappropriable. Ain't no grasping presence to be grasped, no endless fight for standing to withstand, just this anaproprioceptive falling into tangled discord's felt review. Such movement intimates black meta/physics—almost. All in transport all the way up in here, way out from out from out from there, where Harlem is nowhere, in passage, the indexical play of observer and observed, theorist and theorized, dreamer and dreamed, ebbs in topographical caress. Glistening, unheld in gazing, intricate toward gala, neither here nor there we go, down at the cross.

The more we read all that beauty, the more unreadable we are. Transparency tries to hide a grammatical black hole, a (spiraling refusal of) singularity that flares us into visionary company. It all has to do with it, this apposition in the scene, his deposition of scenography. He brings us with what he is and sees, which is us; or, we're brought with them in what he's not and sees through. That embrace, the ecstatic terrain of all that beauty, is Baldwin's function. He's like a telephonic switch in a telephoto lens, seeing double doubly seen through, sounding life but seen with, too, as if three and more + less, mass found in variable densities of blessing, gliding, Jimmy'n'em at study, *todo mundo de Portela*, foretelling, divining that confabulous, alchimeric way we move in camera. His is the eye through which the scene he's in is seen. He stays there, like a loving machine, but on the way, his eyes not now his own in being seen through by the others who can't see but somehow see the fate of all that beauty. All this turbulence comes with "that," which is so emphatically not "this," subventing by subverting some kind of living in our terribleness with hard, delicate extraretrospection. Derivative of "this" in its egocentric particularity, "that" drifts in crowded, nervous torpor. Those hallways go everywhere but gone, but something else is held in something being held off in the making (bending, crumpling) of a dislocation where buddies are and have no bodies. The nearly metaphorical errancy of "that" is there to let us know he doesn't merely look at us. He looks on us, and in that burden, we are covered and unenframed. We live where you and I can't live, which is the truth of all that beauty, which we protect and convey, as lovers.

Where'd he get eyes to see all that like that? Against the grain of the father's desperate and uncertain cruelty, which he never ceased writing about and trying to understand and forgive and indetermine, Baldwin is mama's baby all along. Look how he sees (through) himself in Bette Davis' eyes. What's going to happen to her now? What will happen to all that ugly beauty then? What happens when we murmur, throng, and shudder? There's a wordsheaf arrayed in morbid, experimental want—a wet, atonal burst of seasoned speech as if in every gaze lay the molten structure of another language. All that *enchevêtrement*'s so sharp, so fly, so undervisible, you have to put your sunglasses on so you can feel it, like Elizabeth Eckford. The Little Rock Nine and the Harlem Six and the Little Rock Nine of Harlem swing those wine- and urine-stained hallways; and in preoccupied company, Klook twirls revisionary nightsticks. That's our braille and brushed prosaics. Our shedding shed's the portrait in the sharding of the mirror. Then here come the earth in threads, its nature having risen, its finger optic love come down, hand and eye uncoordinate but social and unbearably inseparable. Relation slides in monkish transposition. Cœnobitic sight off-site, exogamous insight flown off the handle, unowned, uncitable, dispersively excited, exodic jam, all exit all the time in cineballet's shaded glance, grave, ungraven, unworldly, 'cause we're too from the good black dirt, index all anarranged, all frayed in arabesque, pointing fringing back at its own heart, which brings on the juice of our broken flesh, our little broken *Flasche*, our blurred and burled, unoriented surface. The wine, the blood, the shot, the scene, all dance, aw, man, it's all a kind of miracle. Down here with us because he looks like us, because he looks like her, they tell us how to look like them, so we can reach through us to what we share.

come on, get it!

with Michelle Castañeda, Laura Harris, Arthur Jafa, Ra Judy, Julian Moten, Lorenzo Moten, Valerie Cassel Oliver, Elizabeth Povinelli, Denise Ferreira da Silva, and Wu Tsang'n'em

Lorenzo Moten
Humanities C, 3rd and 8th, T/Th
April 18, 2017

XIV

The smile of life is a blackbird.

The blackbird is the creator of a happy living.

You see the sun, a garden, a river. A blackbird shall be seen.

A blackbird brings joy to the world.

Black is the base of a drawing and an art piece.

Black is the color of the sky when stars shine.

Black is my culture and my color.

14.1

This is the world
and here I am and
as I am but not at
all the work is all
and not at all and
all and all and all
and nothing and
Prince says "please

14.2   come" from nothing, from all of
          Zora, in all of Dara,   the world
                                        is dry land,   earth is water.

                                                            Our regular shit is muddy

and irregular. Our shit is the shit, in this regard. Regardless, we started walking the floor of the sea to turn it over, plowing the muck, low, country, just like
mules of the leafy green, sempiternal in sodden underground, thinking the sudden thickness of our steps, infused with periodic swimming to get the air we
can't breathe, saving breath in the muddle of our passage, as Mullen says, or been fixing to say. Fixing we say like f'i'n—imagine a little swelling into place
after the consonant, just a little bit broader time before the x turn to a t, which is implied, then silenced, then acts that same little hollow before the n,
because the end won't come, then one last breath, and keep writing that shit underneath the floor, as our commune. The heavy step of getting down taps
lightly in makeshift repetition, this constantly coming back down beat, m'boom'd in unslit density, recessive unrest in black bottom. The silky, lyric viscosity
of how we move held down—so that all we can do is take the leg, fling limbs in contact, play mas and ball just like the common amputee—is cool

          as the other side of the silty pillow. Our
        shit is irregardless, in this regard.
    That antecitational burst
          is the book of life; and all we got to

              do is come out
        to show you we ain't
    got to show them shit.

We're posthumous and prenatal. The shit is
posthumorous and preternatural. In the muck, the deep on

shore, wading (weighed, waiting), bathing—we laugh to keep from
laughing like a tremendous submachine.

The earthiness of life is irreducibly moist.
Digging is a kind of diving.
Having turned to the turn, we see that shit, we see the shit, we see our shit
and
keep our head above water so we can dive, dig?   Anamphibian,
unarmored,

adrift, underderived

from a prehistory of
fallenness,

black life is wet,

like when Nate tends to certain fluidities of
gait,
but gracefully
mudstuck
in the brutal clearing
of land, unforgetting the river's
memory,
like Morrison says,
in Mississippi,

like Suné
says, when

the escapist
sings

rose at

summer

while

singing

I never learned to

swim

while swimming
down the
broken street.
We're
whales,
and he don't

know

how we
embrace,
submerged as Mary
Lou and
whirled
unworld
as Dar
wish.

14.3

What's it feel like
to see through blackness,
mixing singing and drowning,
sounding and dancing,
but hesitating forever to be
a signal or a judge? This
they asked on holiday,
in protest of themselves,
surrounded by themselves
in bolts of blue, though that
honorable fabric don't feel so good.

Whiteness is the set of
interpersonal relations.
The interpersonal is an
intrapersonal fantasy. The
intrapersonal is an impersonal
fantasy. The impersonal
fantasy of the intrapersonal is
your picture, imagination
in the law of solitude,
on the other hand,

in which this same hand
is held, off blue, in extrapersonal
folding. The image of hands
held in folding (sociality;
blackness) is unavailable but
the tangle (sociality; blackness)
infuses every image. My black
death is my debut, my stole,
done up in blueprint blue,
it sure looks good on you.
It just don't feel so good

14.31

to disappear in a loose arrangement of flowers.

Slave narrative ain't the genre in which one gives an account of slavery and oneself;
slave narrative is the disappearance of oneself and the diffusion of slavery

in the giving, which can't be accounted for, of the account,

sounding drowning's loose arrangement.

14.4   Just be making something all

the time so you can use it
to be making something with somebody
all the time. Maybe the distinction is between impathy and empathy—one emerging
from a point of view, the other occurring in splinter

and entwine, tyrion, terrion, but which knows which
is which; maybe it all goes back to that same
black athenic vehemence and passion,

an infeeling of outness sung
for the caravan. Look how she crossed him. She ain't talking 'bout the game. She
from around the way of ain't no way
and ain't no nonviolent way to look at it. The camera pans down,

moves down, spiraling into the wine and urine-stained hallway.

And what the camera moves toward as eye, I a hand that somehow
was and is the camera,
the hand's
gesture at and with,
in all this beauty as
the camera's motion, its having fallen, in
fallenness, is
all that beauty.

11

15

Whiteness is the set of interpersonal relations,
a tractor beam for the placement of earth,
miscreants trying to put where they live in
their pockets,
                                                                    as we have not and we
                                                                                are not
                                                                    but we share,
                                                                    spacetime sheer
                                                                    in shards, J.B.
                                                                                Lenoir
                                                                    of the lived

experience, black affect's fact, the
                              nor, the (p)anafrican hunch, that
                        mess up the genuine
                                          article.

                              15.1

Resistance is an atmospheric condition whose relation to power, which is derivative
                        of resistance, is derivation itself. Derivation turns relation inside out. Preservative,
                                                            explosive, unrestricted
                                                  endogamy, like a ship upon the sea.
                                                                    We tend

                              to think

antiblackness
is the denial of
personhood to
black persons; it's
also the imposition
of personhood on
blackness. It's
raining man, and I
wish it would rain,
but looking back
on when I
was a little
nappy-headed
boy, back when
we entered black
study, my feelings
begin to get their
exercise elsewhere,
along the road to
my disappearance.

Is there an etymological, and then, perhaps, conceptual, connection between a parent and apparent, chill, zo, so beautiful you let me disappear?

16

Rhythmic placelessness is our garden in folding, bending, and crumpling. Back to living

again, with its inborn recursion, is prophylactic to any future meta/physics, or an ante/meta/physics for a preface that can't stop
coming. We share the preservation of placelessness under the duress of placement.

To be put in place and kept in place; to be conferred a place and to have to have it, to have to own it, to have to try to keep it,
to have a body imposed upon one, as one's place, one's simultaneous foundation and incarceration, in denial of n + one, is monocultural
sugar for your golden bowl. Our *milpa*, all out from and all up under and all over all and all of anyone's ownership of solid,

subdivided ground, turns transubstantiation cosubstantial, *comida, conmovida*, that's not your body, that's my body, as she almost says
she almost says, as there they go all fallen,

all fallen out together, dislocating, differentiating the mass.

The celebration of the mess
in mass displacement, the unruly,
anamonastic dispersion and cœnobitic
diffusion and,
as such, in all
its afformative force, the
preserved and
placeless place, the gateless,
bloodstain'd
gate Wu says black women say
they hear their babies they can't

have be trying to say, the view
they walk, vestibular blur,
be mulebone blue,
deacon

blue, blue
spill for the losers
of the world, which the
soloist, who is not one,
impersonates as
a circular thrill of
floating, recircular field.
Let our flesh be
shared, shar'd, shear,

14

sheeeeeeeeeeeeeeeeeeeeeeeeeeeeeit,
it's hard,
damn,
this quick,
incarnate
incompleteness.

16.1.1

The thing Ra calls the event of the negro is the sign
of reviled, refused, recombinant generality. The sheer
Ellingtonia wrapped around the wooing presence of

the absence in the instrument, which is there in the
presence of the instrument, which is there in the elegant
recess of ark surrounding deep in the edge of sounding,

some of them asking in a migrant chord's embrace about
release, some possible one two that won't take anybody's
fixed position, is some degenerate, satin generativity.

16.1.1.1

Ra says individuation—and the
individual—is not just not one; they are, more
generally, split and supernumerary, some kinda
paired, pared, paraindividuality, an impaired
individuation whose design is
pointed toward a self whose business is in the street,
open, processual, but dignified
at the gig, with that fly-ass gig
bag.
Ra sidesigns "intellect-in-action"
(sighing a favorite phrase of Du Bois playing),
impersonating—
in an open
set of open sets of
unsettled, unsettling,
breathing, handed sheafs—as something other than himself,
which is as it should be, which is how he is,
this continual calling us
out our name, in love with
how we open up somehow
sometimes, rubbing something
in and out of the way
of things, copula all
out of place, portable

15

as the sound we see
in the surround,
Ra says, as he always
be saying, like Baraka always be saying that militant
leather grieve and move and celebrate that we
a mess.

16.2

What if we mess it all up?

Then you can't tell us how to use it. What if the umbrella
underneath which dividual and individual, singular and multiple, severable
and asunder don't quite live is the merely conceptual condition of
separation, which feel so good when you rub up on it that pulse comes to an
end in sheets of reign and killing moon and thin derivative?

Then you can't tell us how we're wrong. What if the
relation between, which is the place between placelessness,
timelessness, and inseparability, is no-count, after all, like B.B.'s
unbearable phrasing on how blue? Can you get to that, sister? Can
time travel on this train?

Then maybe vision is the (hidden) scandal. PIE root *weidh,
"to separate"/ PIE root *weid, "to see," as if to

separate is to see; as if separation is, at first, an ordering of the seen
that

is, more fundamentally, an ordering-in-seeing.   What if to think in disorder, like
Ra, like
Denise's song-flute, is to think outside (ordered) seeing, the sound of that dropped
"h" resplendent in Hester, regiven by Brother?

What if this interplay of ordering and seeing is
solitary confinement? What if disorder is having a
party in the givenness of the party?

Ra plays the companionship of sentient
flesh, thinking in disorder, and experience in sunlit
placelessness till we're all the way out our damn
minds in another storybook in half-leaf shade.

                                                          If the problem is
                                                       the maintenance of

the maintenance of

                                                       separation,

              where you are seen,   I see you,
                        happy now,
                                                                  then
              motherfucker?   saving is the blur
                                                         that movement
                                                         makes in not
                                                         arriving.

16.3

Ra thinks the eventual
   thing as
 irrevocable passage
through embodiment
   as imposition and theft, the trace
 of it in nothingness
              given in withdrawal
from thingliness,
      where grace is constant,
radically anarchic,
groove and furrow
      spiraling.

                                                       16.31

                                                       Perhaps, in this regard, bodies are just remnants of calculation
                                                                      left to the wind of their own captured fading.
                                                              It's like a dam, or a diked-up deictic
                                                              rabbit in Beverly Farms, hoping to be cooked by Beverly
                                                       Corbett, but subject to the subject's description of subjective
                                                       experience, which is lonely, at the base of a tree it never noticed,
                                                       being a b rabbit and silent at the next cypher, thereby constraining
                                                       us to picture and enumerate the subject of experience at the

intersection of the in/di/vidual and the (in/di)visual, is it a rbt or a
dck, dō opn r clsd, fst or thrn, naw,

                                        just this and that cloud
                                        not-in-between
                                        us.
                                                Us, motherfucker. All
                                        anauthentically what.
                        This?
                                That beauty.

17

That dance. Maybe that's all life is, anyway,

that open need of chance. I mean,

Chili says there is no time travel 'cause he's been there.

Mama'n'em'wan'ere'no'mo, he says. He says,
they left an open door, and then it's down
to the direction. A fit between come for me
and please come, he says,

who dead?

Well, look how the dead get down,

                        come on down, we say, as Rankine says we say, so every shade can underhear what Hayden says.

The austere, unlonely office of the homeless is hospitality. Sunday morning, early, coffeeless, orangeless, winter

                        lit up

                        like Ra's
                        late Jb's
                        peignoir worn
                        till sundown.

Naw, we gotta learn to see through things. That's movement, seeing through; gotta learn to love that. Gotta learn to love being seen through. Things are

apparencies, lenses, not like open caskets through american pictures but what, in turning from the illusive, delusional density of that thing, let lovers get

down in the environment. The work is alleyway in its disappearance, when disappearance ain't just vanishing but radical indivisibility that apposes, in
radical presence, the merely apparent. Disapparent, radical presence is dissed appearance; it's like some lotion made of valyrical steel by valerie oliver.

If the art world is just a formal conspiracy to make sure that the nothing that's seen through is detained in things that can only be seen when they're
the only things to see; if what it is to see through radical presence is obscured by desire for the monument, the mirror of the dead, which—with
sound logic and absent morals—identifies inapparent instrumentality as a degraded antagonist; and if the work just wants to be a disappearing passage to

the socioecological plain through white, vampiric omnicide, one by one: then, naw, man, we got to see if we can see through some echomusecological

museology, and anarrange the scene we set, and h'ain't, and see through. Feld's field, Baldwin's scene, undividual, undervisual, felt, relaxed in all that,
accompanied by creek and castanet, while creek and castanet are sung to by Michelle. Why destroy a Schutz when you can destroy a Rembrandt?
I used to know all these people who know how to see through shit. Then, I found myself,
here.

Man is a singularity one all but can't help but believe in but all can do it easy.

19.1

On the other muhfuckin' hand, neoliberalism is a concerted attempt to obscure the essential and essentially exclusionary relation of identity and politics, which is better known as liberalism, which is less well known as fascism, (business) man. It's ashamed of where it comes from, a cold city on a dry marsh. Lots of loose talk about hills and light, and here we come and go, the wet recrudescence of the marsh, the much more + less than malarial life of drops of nonlocal gold, as anti- and ante-aristocratic swarm laid open to natural, natal, univocal return.

Unenlightened, incarcerally free to use politics as a weapon against murderers and their intentions, our primary target is politics. This straight-ahead strait obscures us till, disaggregate and sneaky-clear, freely constrained to use identity against the zombies who invent it, identity is our end. This paradox lets us find ourselves, here. I'm so and so, I'm this, I'm that, huh; but we all just wick-wick-wack, acting like little pullets, lost in the pitter patter of our lil' ol' blank-ass bullets, meddling, middle-brow bullshitters with our trifling, tweedle dumb shit twitter bitterness, our semiprofessional nastiness, our raggedy-ass new spastic pre-black liberality.

We try to protect ourselves from them and forget to protect us from ourselves.

19.2   Why is there something rather than nothing? So devils can steal it.   19.3

Does art move
against our
terrible capacity
to settle? Or does
it settle where

we move? Violence
is all it should be,
nothing but
beauty, till we
say that shit
to the violent air.

The whole in what
we see through
can't be stolen,
ain't my stole,
but what we share.

19.4

The world is a picture. A point of view is a picture's possibility. If one can occupy a point of view, and take a picture, then one can be pictured, too. This reflective picturing in spacetime is Newton's physics and Kant's metaphysics doing the nasty—remover unmoved, can't move, or just not moving all that good. Meanwhile, here's "corrigenda for gayl jones," for Gayl Jones:

Does Corregidora come (to(o))
correct or is she a thing
to be corrected? Can she
bear correction? Must she
bear correction? Is her bearing

alive? Can she bear, as Alex
might say, that orsinic inability
to bear the music we bear?
We got an ear for unbearable
detail, as Alex might say. Can't
stop. Won't stop when we
get enough. Can't call it.
Can't claim it. Ain't mine.
Sing it. Can't say it. Run tell
that degenerate sound,
defective gourd and cold
flow bairn, unbjorn, baby. mama,
come on! Can't come, son.
Won't come. It's a cold, cold
coming. It's like ice
around my heart. I know I'm gonna quit
some body. Every time this
feeling starts we done made us
some connections. Done made us
some corrections. We cut
your hard and lonely will
off. We wound your death
and play that back as more
than just not you. This you?
Naw, this not just you, my
beautiful sister. Black is so
much more than just not you
it hurts. Gimme more, gimme
more, I want it, I like it.
Party on fire, then I'm gone.
Nothing to correct
'cause it's all connected.

Slave song ain't properly oppositional because it ain't properly
autobiographical. All it tells is nobody's story, assuming the apposition, generation
after impossible generation,

19.41

as "disguise" coolly reveals itself, the concealment of identity misunderstood in the disavowal and placement of appearance,

covered in a kind of uncovering, the mutual orbit of concealment and
unconcealment, confinement and revelation, hiding and showing, uniform and

monstrosity, bad habit, strange habit, off inhabitation.
Nonrecognition was the world burning; the ice cap started melting in the hold.
Antiblackness ain't personal but is it experienced personally? Is such experience real? Or true? Naw, it's way more fucked up than the real thing.

Ain't nothing like that, as Aretha say they say, something like beautifully nothing
like Marvin and Tammi say they say it.

Works of art are to be seen but art only works if it's seen through till it's gone. Hey, 19.5, no, we got nothing in common; no, we can't talk
at all; but when we slide on down, our queerness, our hard, gemlike black bitchiness, our nothingness, is our opacity, our opulent

transience, our flamelike,
opalescent train, lil' rose.   To be seen through can't help but move, but we can't help it, that's all we do, quilt flesh and earth,
unmanned in lil' walter's harm and matter
and whisper in bent study, rocking steady, everybody steady rocking till everybody gone.

It's like a book of gauze for which cinema prepares us; but we don't return to
the book, we turn through its disappearance. The dance of the turn and fold bears
cut and tear, which

ain't about rendering things transparent but enacting the lucence through
which we see no things. We see through things—a book of glass, a black-

stained color wheel and violate sash in abreactive brush and broken, turning, ana

redactive loosening of
leaves. They gone, that's what it feels like, that's what we feel now. Let's call

this song exactly what

it is—a retha'd

array of look off shudder,
view off point and vibed, shook wander, indeterminate tremé

delirium, studious in ain't studying you nonchalantly, breathing a little subtle-
ass, unsettling distance and then some, an inseparable beauty not even
art can take. All that.

20

Regarding this disregard, black art is criticism in the afternoon,

sun and shade

with Roy DeCarava'n'em

Blackness is the ceaselessly miraculous demonstration that there is no black and white, just sun and shade. This insight is serial, over and over, all over the place, as an irreducible element of art consciousness's remedial education, registering the condition that is without remedy. Photographs of people continually getting over the fact that they can't get over reveal their terribly beautiful inability to get over the fact that they do, which is given in looking back in mournful wonder, ahead in worn anticipation. Insofar as the photograph looks back and forth like that in general, its existential condition is given when blackness in play, as the play of sun and shade, is playfully, painstakingly regarded.

The capaciousness of black's color field is actualized out from the outside, all in all, all this insight forming outside inside out. Efforts to achieve black's purity misunderstand its depth of study. In documenting play's concrete abstraction, where abstraction folds in flown documentation, given understandings of abstraction therein unfolded, unraveled, hand delivered, put in play, black is an all but gray blue university—the contemplative eclipse of portraiture and its substructural meta/physics that sociality convenes. It's like a detail in Brueghel that Brueghel left out; or something left out in Brueghel and recovered from and in its immersion in a terrible, projective, illuminating solution of silver and gelatin. Particulate dispersion is applied in the interest of monstrous, ecstatic showing. Faces are held between torn up and hiding, grostesquerie and umbrage. That's our nonparticulate disbursal. The development of excluded essence is a tragedy you render miraculous. What it is to look at black as black, all up in all of it so emphatically that in its absence color is everywhere, is where you carefully, playfully, unsettlingly reside.

What is it to reside without settling? Is that is or is that ain't like being stuck in sweetness, held in life? Black life is like Ife in hell, or on the el, which is the sound of joy, Sun says. Sun who? Son House, I think, unhoused some day in Harlem's bright Mississippi, two little boys drawing out that string in strange, strung out fray. See, their play is fraught, insistent movement, nervous muscularity, mobility that stays, that's all but still, but for the shift in (over)tone. Captured motion's constant flight turns out to always sound like something. The shit is eerie enough for the difference between loud and quiet not to signify. Silence and blackness are more + less than one in this regard, which is often disregarded as the train falls through the trees, the skyscrapers, and everything, and nothing. The sound you see is movement, a resonance of back and forth in falling from partition to partiality, a preference for our social incompleteness, individuation played out, relation exhausted, in obscure, tensile revelation held right here: "Ahhhh. What's happ'nin'?!! What's happ'ninnn? Shit, I know sump'n's happenin'—'cause everything's movin. Baby." Everything's gone. Every photograph is a photograph of that, which an actual photograph of that makes deafeningly clear. It's not that it's not a sin and a shame that *Sun and Shade* is so beautiful. It's just that black, in being so beautiful, is foregiveness.

a turn

with John Akomfrah'n'em

To spill the frame and auditorium, it turns into a problem of the turn and not the cut,

                              the blue traversal when we fall, point of entry

point of view's displacement,

cut just to let the page (re)turn, like that old way of reading through incision, cut so it can turn in cursive torsion, twist and shout

out to the open book, the verso, *el converso*, of the turn(ed) into a common place of turning, the murdered refuge of the world,

the scarring of the story, the story of the score in fractured

rounding, the terrible chance of her global positioning, her *insouciance*,
dutch mastery's resistant animation

tuned in burning. Turned

in blur's serration, in serially unfinished conversation, her contrafactive forcing, the music of the water,

                                 look how we turn the history of the turn, in the co-presence of the page, in the two places at
once, for the nonlocality.

        You can't get here from here, and no one ever really comes and goes in this endless homelessness.

The cinema of the open book of the common place is a general amniosis. It all but won't be cinema, after all, all sinned against in cinematic sinning,

                   the fluid absolution

                      turned in binding, in terrible refusal of beginning, inseparable in surf and
rain and circling seizure,

                    serving,

                    turning, in the break of our unbroken act of faith.

receipts from *A Recital for Terry Adkins*

with George Lewis'n'em

throatflung   anepic   rage through floathrung
       range   anthemic   jumprung   unprehensile
apprehensive   turnthrough   grasping   north
  through twisting   to perceive through grasping   sense

 in letting go   in you   in it   obscure   but lit in
anheroic   view   ulu unsung   through
     intuition   at black night   in nutjuitok
   and   larry   clark is   passingthrough

the sun. In Nanjemoy, you cannot own, a polestar but a cabin boy, but then first man and then first one, though turning shell and twisting through, through strange returning, you ain't one. The strange attraction, as it shifts, magnetic, unmagnetic, in degrees of ice and hugged in fold and flipped, in enigmatic ceremony all the time, in throatsong, and ululative throatslash, and let you in their language. Their language let you in, and let you go, and, estuarine, ecstatic, circumpolar but straight down, then tideflung, flown around a central thren that disappears into their language.

He had a black snowmobile. He drove
out under the northern lights. His carpet
was a northern shawl. The precision

of his phrase displacement, because invitation
and demand write through each other
with each other to be for what it is

to wear the cold as shelter,
which is what we do on the ragged edge of thickened
water everywhere, was everywhere.

Absolute on the ragged edge of work
and love and then to bear that shelter into falling air
and share it in a vocal game of jew's harp

and frame drum or if he only dance to breathe
irregular at last in black square, or Clinton Hill,
or between here and various Dunbar Arms,

or if Usir himself can raise up in the studio
or lay that long horn through the various ice,
offering to listen, listen, and understand

the sandtide and raise us up in various circle
and El-Dabh. The dead are warmed by absolute
prayer. Ra's setlessness is early, frozen song
and some question regarding where you live
and who you are. Some concern about
the residency of the kind one. Some
restlessness with naming the residual
kindness in how you live and where you
live. Some tendency to reset the koan
of restless rest and snowrise, that it was
only frost, that it was just the curling air
of black's release of portraiture, the recitation
of the moan of faceless face, placement and
naming in honorable outline but for thingless
residual, revision off to the side and shit,
re re re re re re re like Aretha'n'em every day
for every day. Now, what's a natural woman
singing every natural thing got to do with this
optic white mythology of muse and drone?
Some kind of way of thinking black feeling.

It's not that we're
not advanced in
the quickness of our
chemistry. It's not
that we're not kind,
or that we don't bear
the way we're carried
in our own story. It's
not that we don't also
always need to be
telling you who we
are and that this ain't
also always the way
we tell you that who
we are is all but you
when you violently
tell us who you are.
It's just that it's a
little bit more like
that underneath it all,
and so it's not like that
at all, that's all. In
villanello's ear for
reels of moor and
cold unwintering,
there's another living
on that's paradise.

All this heroic rising above not
hearing and this rising in absolute
north against the grain of that
counter-heroic background against
the grain is all supposed to be off
minor, all off the wall of heroes.
Recital just wants to be against
the grain of all that; it's supposed
to fall off all that in asking, what are
we doing? Regarding all this re-
covery, what the fuck is all that?
What the fuck are we doing? Are we
gonna lose all of what we found
in loss in all this hoarding and citing?
All this homeless, residual snow
and ash? All this drowning and
motionless water? All this grasping
of all this little all we got? All this
absolute falling and asking and asking
again in rolling thumpexpression through
nonnoncarrownic koan through and
through? It's like the will to adorno:
a history of freedom in unfreedom in
sprung fingering come to ask again,
come on man, can you come ask again?

shepherd of bells
martyr of sweet
prophet of wool
soldier of bees

shadow of bird
mystic of sweat
prisoner of wind
servant of blue

take ecstasy with me.

symphony of combs

with Susana Baca, Satch Hoyt and Victoria Santa Cruz'n'em

They yelled at me, Black! Black Woman! They called me Black Woman and I called myself saying don't call me out my name. I'm Black! I said. I'm a Black Woman and my sons and brothers shout it, dance it, claim it, caught up in the rhythm of reciting, their hip and hip tight movement turning, twisting how freedom and agony surveil each other everywhere, mess up every messed up everywhere in sowing that fold and cut they carry. They send a primal scene whose white mask'd repetition is cooked down low to rope and clothe the one-line force of *soy*. I am whatever you say I am, but not the way that you say I am, 'cause that's the way that I have to be, if you wanna come on after me, when said in concert comes uncountable as hair's new groomed and grooved refusal to uncurl. *Me Gritaron Negra!* Here they go right now.

Negra soy! is our song of ascents, they say. Here we go right now. Where we been, been where we at. Here, we bear that we been there in never having been there and the other way around. Our rising fallenness is scraped off contact, layered shift and feel, release. Remain. Refuse. Remain. removed, what we do we do over till what's done is undone in haptic, anilluminative halo. What's that resound(ing) sound like? In echo of that sideways lean, they say, here go some sonicartographic do. Fifteen black women from Cali, dressed in various shades of white, walk barefoot through a curving ray of microphones and start to comb their hair. They start to comb their hair like it ain't no thing. They start to comb their hair and say, which one?

How hair get did are ways of violent care. A tightened left of traces give in taking shape. Hair's rich internal rant—it's frizzy way to be on fire, flaring up against every act and condition(ing) of regulatory burning, or relaxational frying, or alchemical dyeing and side-lying, or everyday bed-riddenness, or them all but impossibly articulate folios of wraps—recites some prior resistance. Malleable crunchiness and cut off crispiness bear percussive implications. A choir of rubbing, crinkling and pulling free flee countlessly.

Mapping turns to echotopographic dislocation, which exceeds him in the nonperformative pretension—the seductive presumptuousness—of the women he fixes, who won't stay fixed, displacing his conduction with unfurled anautonomy. He almost stays unfixed with all of them. It's not that they form a body that knows itself in knowing the precise relations of its parts. It's more like a feel whose real airiness in density gives the restrictive illusion of body away. Here, tender-headed tinder-headedness is more + less than individual emplotment. It's a general dance the drummer taps into while lining out ensemble's independence of limbs—that light, thick booming in percaressive chorale, auricular tining and teasing, orchestral scratch. Satch ain't so much head arranging for a band as setting up ritual conditions for various resurrective enactments, or circumatlantic surrogations, of anoriginal insubordination on the cross. In this regard, combing bears *una historia de la reveuelta negra*.

Having long been a dj, well-subversed in the art of the record and what it holds in being cut off from live performance, when the object disappears every day in Mary's weeping fog, Satch works a kind of phantom limn, blurring the line between impairment and augmentation, analysis and mimesis, tilling and diving. Performance records this loss and finding, which is handed on in the recording of their performance, like making place in seeing through. When lyric breakdown acts like preening, in disruptive enhancement or retouching or overdubbing, as if to show some essence of the natural, where position is some viciously non-localized tangle, you comb it out, or cut it off, and know it's gon' recur. This active nappiness—the torn collusion and far-flung togetherness we keep feeling—is called diaspora, which is the cozy, kilsonian condition that hair describes, sonically mapping the migration it bears and within which it's propelled, repulsed and desired. Here, there, it's shift, not place, that's mapped, place having been locked and twisted in the restive statelessness of arrest within which movement, and what moves, and what is moved, are all but held. What moves moves with and against itself in deformative formation—braided, swept, as in the staging of a beauty shop as public sound booth turned to and in the retracing of halted steps and sunken strokes. Choreography is foregiven in brushwork's blakey rasp, a constantly inconstative, pluperformative utterance discovered, now, as a symphony of combs. A comb is like a harp, in this regard, and a symphony of combs is a symphony of psalms insofar as the comb is sung to by the hair it pulls, screamed at by what it teases. Its plucking is basic, out of the depths, so you can you hear the harm in harmony. Combing is ritual chanting of the psalter, a song of the song of ascents in descents and dissent, ours only because it's not and gone, out from under the proper and the private dubbing one another in brutal redundancy, knotted in praise of the general tangle, I and I against I fanned out in flamed amazement and shook foil, shining ire in the fringe between comb and hair, the teeth of freedom iterative and irritant, itinerant, unacquired, fluted as the exteroceptively interoceptive instrument that knows all Satch's stops, as he would wish, his genius their iration, his arrangement of them anarranging all of him and all as some gilt white roses.

Negra soy becomes *Negra presuntuosa*, in and out of grasp. Seductive Black Woman, Presumptuous Black Woman. Black Woman, in your authentic and essential pretentiousness, your deep and fundamental nonperformance, are you not? Are you nothing other, all? Called out of your namelessness into a general naming, called out on the street where you live, calling out to your name between your street and my soul, called out your name, something of mine is lost where something of yours is hidden; in the rhythm you hand to my accompaniment, my arrangement disappears. How can we fall through what naming and unnaming bears, mystery, who won't be one, or free.

folded moments

with Soo Kim'n'em

Here's a tassel for your book, to join unfinishing; a little nothing in an open knot. That's your form, in a tousling of your book, which is a tassel. Not to be untidy but to cut design in knotted openness. Not to mess up but to comb, informally. No sparring, no tussle, just embrace, a contactual agreement on a bookmark that all but moves.

Your illuminated photography, the botticellian infrastructure of your trees, blurs up close in grid offline. The enhanced scaffolding of your bottle trees is an inner overlay so far outside that placelessness is set on a prepared table. The surface of the sheet is played on like a prepared piano. The on in "played on", in being played on, implies disruptive (re)touch, manipulate mitosis. What's subject to this violent caress, this growth, this all but biochemical incursion, paper worked with an image-moment's infusion and degradation only to be worked and worked again in repetitions of cutting and pasting, bending and straightening, wearing and weathering? Softening and pliability are induced in the breaking of adhesions, the slicing of leaves. Pleats Please, sings the goddess of folds. Pli, Plea, Plié, shouts the godfather of soul, falling to the floor like an open fringe, mellow in microsurgical feel.

Your analchemical city's favela'd metastasis. Landscape burled in ruined augmentation. Flayed polis, delayed layout, skeletal ornament, post-constructive imposition, Reykjavik adorned in adobe like an interclimatic hem, its jewel-encrusted roofs made appropriate to new, unnatural weather. When the infrastructure is a caress, like a pillowed aura that holds the city up, then what holds the city up is the commune. Then, the history of the city waits for us like a spiral: lattice, shred, volumination; blueprints after some living; replacement planes. That taped, mondriaanic dimensionality that undoes the work at the rendezvous of victory, boogie, and incompleteness, incompleteness meaning both more and less than complete, means your work is incompleat, angled, base foregrounded, then removed, for breathing.

You talk about cutting away some of the legibility of the photograph, and that's to fasten, layer, and fold where laceration and discharge are resident complexities, a surrealization of the photographic object that's not bound up with hidden meaning, but commuted in a material content that's not revealed but presented in new construction. Revelation ain't the right word. Deliverance is the right word. Deliverance in veer, as refreshment. A layer is discerned, and removed, then placed on top of the place it left. That's the photograph where they found sculpture, then freed it on ventilated terraces, then fled. Pregnant upon disappearing with "deliberate slowness," incision and insertion reunited after long, false division, entassled but not separate, tessellations that are, as you say, too round to frame.

Tiling, tilling, the trace of aspiration stays on top of what's been layered over air's ectopic presence. Tiling air made out of tilling air. Disjoint open sets in plane-filling arrangement of plain figures. A plain-song of muted twisting like a paper piece. Some contrapuntal lamination of patterns against mastery. When tiles overlap, or blur, is it still tessellation? You finger-comb the photographic plane, tropicalizing very large disarrays made suitable for overhearing, perryscratching the surface of things in counteramish plainness; a plying, soulful, friendliness of the plane

> making skeletal clumps like blood
> ulmer, or cecil's long-sung clustural
> city of serpents, panache and fuzz, or
> some fast-twitch strum and battery,
> some kinda smokey, seconded emulsion

cutting away contextual sky, so if the blueprint comes after the building's been inhabited—if it's worn like a garment, its fabrication rendered incomplete in its becoming-fabric, in its having been texturalized—then what's the time of the photograph? What's the photograph's moment if, in being a blueprint, it comes before what's been photographed? The photograph, even of the out and gone, is an always anticipatory afterlife, living given in covering aeration, in endearing crease, in excisive and endowing reference.

The open book.

The endless

folding

of the moment.

sudden rise at a given tune

with Wu, Tosh, Zo, Chill, Josh Johnson, Asma Maroof, Patrick Belaga and Ligia Lewis"n'em

Droning a drowsy syncopated tune,
Rocking back and forth to a mellow croon,
I heard a Negro play.

Langston Hughes, *The Weary Blues*

As, however, we rise in the realm of conduct, we note a primary and a secondary rhythm. A primary rhythm depending, as we have indicated, on physical forces and physical law; but within this appears again and again a secondary rhythm which, while presenting nearly the same uniformity as the first, differs from it in its more or less sudden rise at a given tune...

W. E. B. Du Bois, "Sociology Hesitant"

How can violence be such a balm? The criminal animation of a more than natural law, anajuridical movement in theater's interstitial space, an experimental acting out of anchoritic cell and cause. The secret life of things is open—made plain, phenomenal ding-hiss, this thing we are, all these things we are, all this, all we keep trying to get to, all we can't get back to, all miles ahead in nothingness is all that's left. Maybe the problem is simply looking at, which is to say listening to. How can you show the out circularity of that perception, its difficult pleasures of (re)turn and syntax, its embedded, imperceptible hesitations and miniature seismic events, its pulsive touches, its (dys + hyper) lexic scratches and scars?

What is slave language? What's it mean to be published? Does displacement make me play the agent of my displacement or does it let me murder my ideal? What if lyric poetry regurgitates identity? Then Phillis Wheatley is fresh, and flesh, and fly as rumination's syndrome. Psyche is the residue of her (in)digestion, which is nurture. Rumination wanders, a resuscitative essay on the run, but you never get there, all that heavy Plymouth plantation peculiarity, voluntary, involuntarily on trial, on edge, over the edge and curved, scooped, sloped, depressive, manic. T is musical, a one note/one pulse percussive flight of emphatic dig like I ain't going antywhere. Authentic mantic gesture is I and I ain't going nowhere. Who you looking at falls to where you looking from, when you looking. Ask and you can cut when and where. You can not remember where or when. You can trace the genealogy of Baldwin's eyes with a little piece of rough silk to get the tactile sense of something going on. It's like Chili cussing out Siri again. It's like when Arendt writes to Jaspers: "I've begun so late, really only in recent years, truly to love the world." Within a certain relegation to the private, given in the form of rescue, this can only be expressed in a sealed envelope, or whispered with deviant love to your rose-gold avatar. Baldwin says there's "something ironic and violent and perpetually understated" in Chili's speech. It's "something tart...authoritative and double edged." Something you hear whenever you hear a Negro play like Langston. It's almost like being in love for those who have never been covered, or born in distress, or have no toposociological hitch, no quantum sociological pause, no subatomic/subspace sliiide.

Feeling sweet feeling drops from my fingertips. The tips imagine autoexcessive caress and come from that imagining. They dance into the scene and the difference in dancing through seeing is inseparable. Hearing saves the place it makes by changing. They prepare a table by twisting, stretching and wrinkling. Gluing and tearing can't be excluded from remorseless working. What it is to taste mass in the heart of eccentricity. What it is, celebration shot down, unburied, unrisen, listening and looking, hearing and seeing, till one another fly away. I wish I could caress. Turn myself off and go on down.

Used to run into this kid at Doe. We'd be browsing the stacks on the top floor, looking at books that explore the frontier between mathematics and philosophy, circling ideas of mathematical existence, or notions concerning the "reality" of mathematical objects—courting black study where continuity, compactness, connectedness, the active sounding of our spooky distancing, nearing, overlap, is a way of walking down the street in love. If there's that divinatory thinking that Oskar Becker calls "mantic phenomenology," then maybe there's a mantic disposition that puts the phenomenological consensus out on the floor, turning, like never to return. What's the relation between fugitive monasticism and the paradisiacal garden? What's the relation between the paradisiacal garden and a hard row to hoe? What's the difference between Moses the Black and Black Moses? What's the difference between Harriet Tubman and Isaac Hayes? Is the theft of stolen moments some new asceticism? Is there an aesthetics of the trans, substantial feast? Angela Davis is our beloved. Our otious lingering is erotopology by an ice-blue stream, like shelves of noise in curve and recess, like the continual forming of a pit. When people move, they move topologically and topographically, meditating through the duet towards o, the open cell. It's not that o comes first; it's that it comes to fuck first up. Hey Tosh! Hey Josh! Form a pit of iterative presences in a field; grass cat-tapped down in swirled squares, little phantasmagoric agoras of rubfall. Earth makes place through world where we hold where study, strain through set logic, stack cruising, till after thirty years he whispers, "Zalamea."

A drum is a woman's club. All the symbols are double envelopes and difference engines, bringing in the sheaves of palm and olive, the innumerable bundles of ointment and anointment that render every unit cecilian and impure, mouths filled with the south in streams, coming virtually through themselves like murmuring birds that get here before they leave there, which they theorize as a new bouquet, a newspaper called the mystery, a project taking shape and losing it, giving shape away with sharp turns and jumped back, homotopic kisses off schedule, margins at the center of their thought, which gloriously falls, to preserve all that sheavy breath in lapsed concentration by deforming it, like a quartet for the end of time's live stream. And where matter is present in nothing, like a fade of porches, leaps in and through the leaves, in the cyrilleization of its seriality, daniel hamm announces a method for the torture of mothers. Black ink is blues blood in manifold, breeze blood in imaginary axes, phase systems out of spiritual linen, rhythm sections out of silk, some pulse fabric in caressive trapfield in a bruised description of this skein of this continuity, silt animated, exhausted, like a choir come out of paper in a reading from the book of thunder, streams in the mouth of florida and more, biscuits of air let go in bursts of handshear, sheaves of sheaves raised up like leavened stone. Don't cite black women. Recite black women. Their doubt percussion, their sister tour, their heavy water.

That's the communicability of the shu. Rather, he made himself nothing by taking the very nature of a servant, being made in human likeness, in the whipping machine, through its power to individuate. They kill him every day and grace is everywhere in fasting. The florescent asceticism of the sheaf. Giving is everything and more, that's all, that's all, the exhaustive communicability of the shu. He was blessed and cursed with visitors. The terrible aestheticism of the sheaf. They came with plates, and tea, in the name of the Crenshaw Legal Clinic. They came as violent, lonely mothers. The essential habit of assembly in a blue concert. The fleet communicability of the shu. The tortured imperative to rest in power. Primordially empty space is in the mix. Come levy rents here if you can. The perfect astigmatism of the sheaf. What harmonizes things, and what's awry in them, all sharing middle distance, nothing different, all the same, at a sudden rise, in the endlessly anarhythmic way we stave off starving. That's the communicability of the shu.

the general balm

with Suné Woods, James Gordon Williams, Etymology Online and Joseph Diaz'n'em

<u>limn (v.)</u>
early 15c., "to illuminate" (manuscripts), altered from Middle English luminen, "to illuminate manuscripts" (late 14c.), from Old French luminer "light up, illuminate," from Latin luminare "illuminate, burnish," from lumen (genitive luminis) "radiant energy, light," related to lucere "to shine," from PIE *leuk-smen-, suffixed form of root <u>*leuk-</u> "light, brightness," clyde'n'em'dam'near alight in strange unlike, the figurative sense of "portray, depict" first recorded 1590s. Related: Limned; limner; limbo.

<u>limnology (n.)</u>
study of lakes and fresh water, 1892; see <u>limno-</u> + <u>-logy</u>. The science founded and the name probably coined by Swiss geologist François-Alphonse Forel (1841-1912). Related: Limnological; limnologist. Hymnology. Line out. Baptize.

<u>arpeggio (n.)</u>
1742, from Italian arpeggio, literally "harping," from arpeggiare "to play upon the harp," from arpa "harp," which is of Germanic origin (see <u>harp</u> (n.)). Related: Arpeggiated (1875); arpeggiation; arpregnably little walter in lit water.

<u>asymptote (n.)</u>
"straight line continually approaching but never meeting a curve," 1650s, from Greek asymptotos "not falling together," from a- "not" (see <u>a-</u> (3)) + assimilated form of syn "with" (see <u>syn-</u>) + ptotos "fallen," tpopos, unassimilated fold of sin in infinite series of sine, krinein, verbal adjective from piptein "to fall," from PIE root <u>*pet-</u> "to rush; to fly; to cut" Related: Asymptossing, turning, tuning, whining, crine, diving, angled, icarine and never wrong and always almost not all there like a detail, so that all we can do is take the leg, and wail to sea.

We bear the atmosphere. How can we carry on? Lift across what lies between, spun by an engine that can't be between, 'cause that's how near we are. We near as difference can be, which is absolutely near. Nothing is all that comes between us

to dance how we cut stevie. The history of weather is the closer we fall apart. The further we go we come to nothing like stevie come to donny in the common vamp. You and I keep violently conquering the nothing that comes between us

as we swim in brackish waters. Lady be lagging good, lovely, (not) going, (don't) go, go, gone in the difference, if there is any, but it still be going on, fallen in a dream we have when we be falling, right there, that little off we keep between us

is a passage we love. Resident hum invisible to the traveler, rubbing actions and events in flicker, loa beholding media in versioning, in always middle traveling, samiya freshening the field and then I'm fading into nothing comes between us.

I am, as I am typing, right now, right here with you as we are reading, doing this very *Invisible Man*nish, Ben Hallish, Bonnie Jonesian kinda thing, playing "But Not for Me," staggered then looping then surging, on YouTube, on iTunes, in the room, till trio turn six and niño, crine. It sounds so beautiful, don't you agree?! He says, "It's all about love" and it's cool, too, 'cause the density of the music increases, but at a rate no greater than that of the music's jamalian lightness. More place is made through being taken at the same time! Kinda like the effervescence of the water when she be swimming towards the end of *The Escapist*. Her fleshly displacement doesn't create more water but more surface under the water. More surface and more suns,

the way musicians breathe in blocks of open breath, blocks like bombshells filled with violets, intimacy and anonymity, and apposition and arpeggiation, all up under that blanket like Papa Jo'n'em. That's a block chord difference in the din of golina'n'em and love is violet incompletion—note erosion and ricochet. What if flesh is the anticipatory arpeggiation of the body, like when Trane plays the solo, and then the head, on "Countdown"? Prior immersion preceded by flight, and Freddie Green sat tight, in open tuning,

extending submersion's extended subversion and doolooped drumming in swimming page to page. The rhythm of the stroke is fly and polyamorous, signifying more + less. Commit to that, in refusal of this, free from one, body let go, ohio fired, pour some water on me. An arpeggiation of the corps and its solitude, which was imposed, having been made to take place, having been put in its place. Our owning bears the wound of being owned, to deepen being borne in empty gestures, reciting this probing that deepens as it can't go deep enough and our hands arise. Black olograph be off, in this respect. Almost misspelled, almost off type, near bewitching, all but off key, we fly away, or float on, or keep on movin', like a fuse, on certainty, or security.

That's just sharing danger, not settling for the envelope, no room, man, no groundstanding, you fucking murderer. Immersion ain't gon' go nowhere. It's inescapable, hence escape's constancy, which bears our movement in being moved. You can't stop it; you can't be it all by yourself. Immersion ruptures solitude no matter what. Even when I'm by myself I'm not. I'm sinking. Intimacy is the joint production of an air pocket the sun sprays; and we manage to look so beautiful in our absolute refusal of orthodoxy in the habitat, in our joint circular breathing. Our circular breathing is why the joint is jumping. And all you can do is kill us; you can't even get us on the phone,

these notes documenting the process, commenting on the product, thereby displacing it, diving in it, turning in it, turning it over, overtoning it, funkily moving and removing it, digging it up, trying to get down with it, word block
corresponding to her structure, and her rupture of that structure, word block all material.
All I gotta do is listen, look, and then I'm gone, but tracing,

like how the sunken city writes the undersurface of the water in *Neveryóna*. And I know somewhere there's a creasing of the water on the shore. We illuminate the water, illustrate it from below, submarginal, sublalian, somehow. Too much water renders the land unprofitable. We swamp thangs, like Nat Turner. What if swimming is choreohydrography—not synchronized but syncopated, independent limbnology, reading what leaves leave in the water, lining out that murky analibrium, xenographic hum, analogic mud, xenographic hug, analogic none, jesus bug treading but hydrophobic but all hydroptique, then drapetomaniacal an underwater placegraph in suspense. Our shit is limbnologically phantophonographic, wheeeee, the black study of the water music. Our life is neither dead nor alive. Nobody wants it but us nobodies, become the water in our whorldliness, the way Cecil loves the word whorl, pullin' like Pullen + Aretha, our watery, pianistic whirlpoolism, falling feeling like running in Bud Powellism, fluidity, but not against, but not for me, but shacked up with solidity, the muck of orchestral furniture in blanketed embrace, worn, donned, put on, puttin' on, showing out, not sublime but ridiculously beautifully just a little bit touched. Our poco nonlocal existence is submarine and subterranean and subparticular. Our atmosphere—the generally relative mama put in play, like Fernando says Angela says, in and all the fuck out the way of the storm too long—is waving. We feed and breathe by touch and sing songs the way Cedric the Entertainer say Nathaniel, that faded l at sundown, in disordered, interminably black and anaiolic Oakland, at the Calvin Simmons Theater, May 15, 1987, in preservation of the antological tonality.

Is there a relation between alienation and arpeggiation? Distanciation and differentiation, as in différance? Chords fall apart. Together, we fall apart to here in there. What if here there are no persons, only chords in various (anti-)states of throwing down? What if blackness is just the theory and practice of throwing down? Our music troubles the water. Our dancing troubles the music. Our music and our dancing trouble the body into inexistence. We worry lost body till they flesh again. We worry worry worry. Cheryl Wall be standing up beside, back against, and back up off. Can't quite let nothing go or be.

We harp on the water. Our register is infinitely low. The face of the deep, in the fear of the water. Unportraited, before time, high water everywhere.

But not for me
twice,
          staggered, looping,
it's cool, too, 'cause the density
is light, phonic sparkle,
                    reversed countdown.

Flesh ropes the body it waits for,

                         when three
threads out and fans and brushes

          in duress of emplotment
in possession,

                         immersion
ruptures solitude no matter what.

We can't breathe forever.

                    We look
for air pockets—an informal market
on the corner, the club, a chapel
made of bottle trees.

               Every last
breath we want to breathe
somebody,   so beautiful in refusing,

graphic in quartering ourselves,

                    ana solid
in embrace.

Wasn't nobody but some chords
in various antistates and jingles.

Blackness is arpeggiation
and displacement.

Blackness is swimming,

can't quite let the water go or be,
                we harp on the water.

The blackness of the whole thing
is that our flesh lights up the world,
the ringing, the bubbles,

                the particles appear
to fade
in suspense. What else
might happen to us folds us
in. Not, but amniotic wail.

                We're whales.

We hate the world. We love
the word whorl, our whirlpool
pianism, our pullen, our
pullin', our practice,

                                our
        saturated name.

index

with Lauren Berlant and Kathleen Stewart'n'em

There's too much pointed repeating to point at, being caught up in it. The overall is all over the place, numberless in thick and thin. No place to go is all over the place. Shifters, riffless because the splits are staggered, get their drink on. Echoes can't get located, obvious things gone aviary, map flown all over the place. We're missing the overall. You're missing the overall,

this way free that way, green, stuck way out like this, when don you know de day's erbroad? Outnumbered, parenthetical finger pointing around the corner, won't straighten all up in can't straighten how you straighten up in the morning, all your voices unravelling while your voices lounge in the overall, what pleasure had these tracks laid down? Nothing but all that shifting,

how the road turns over the edge of anything you be trying to do. Let's call this song exactly what it is. In lieu of its name let's call it you, or y'all. All y'all up in there started flying all over the place, started missing, started can't get started, won't fly right, can't get it straight, can't turn it loose but there it go and now it's gone and there y'all go, can call it but can't point to it.

Y'all keep saying that's what I'm talking 'bout don't even sound right and now you want an index? And that's just what y'all be always talking 'bout with all the voices in your voices and their outstretched hands. The overall is alert to this dancing more than singing, y'all said, and there's a hand jive with some presence in it all throughout but no place special, off to the side,

glancing at all the colors in thirty-third. Level, degree, resource flicker back and forth all over the place, amarillo all over the place as sunlight, called exactly what it is but pointed out only so we can say what it feels when we describe it, get it all down to the point of it being all y'all all over the damn place. It feels terribly beautiful. It feels terribly beautiful everywhere y'all go.

Been watching the pot, paying close attention to texture, but with resistances that turn to ambivalence if you tend to them. The cook's resistance to her food is intensified by her presence in the pot. She's in the soup but not of it, being off in it. The trouble with selflessness is that it appears to be a function of absolute self-absorption. You give yourself over to what you endure, rubbing slowly through the pillar of that band running down your leg; otherwise, more people would try to take it up. You gotta have a theory of it, see it from somewhere, evidently. So, it's better to chip away at your point of view with the extreme care of the merely culinary, submitting to your own bitter flavor, than it is to go ostentatiously hungry.

impromptu, t(o)ba
with

Lauren Berlant, Kathleen Stewart, Andrew Causey, Susan Lepselter, Stephen Muecke, Ben Anderson, Renee Gladman, Barbara Browning, Imre Lodbrog, Ben Anderson, Anjali Arondekar, Kris Cohen, Chicu Reddy, Hal Sedgwick, Ken Wissoker, Edgar Garcia and Denise'n'em

To be announced is tough (on) black asses, as in what's in the soup and what the soup is. Now, it's on. The serpentine chitlin' circuit is like a trip in an audience with no friends. It's not that there are no friends; it's that it's not enough for us to be friends. No time, where did it go, everywhere, not even after hours. I guess I have to capitalize "is" as there's exception in the ordinary. The ordinary exception is all lover. The place, Lyotard and the difference, where the truth resides, between language and metalanguage, is Tarski made frank, *Francuski*, really. *Schnee ist weiss ist wahr si la neige est blanc*, a soup of snow, or fog, the general turbulence, or turmeric, or your turn.

To be announced, I guess, is what I am. I guess I want to be announced. I can't just walk into the room any kinda way. But fuck the assignment. I ain't doing it. I don't like exercise(s). My back hurts. My back is broad and we don't do no worlding. Ain't me, ain't mine, now what? And I won't not do it by myself, either—not even here. I don't want to be a person among other persons. I don't like that kind of hovering. I can't accede to the fact that this is my life. But this did happen to me and I want to say that somewhere, in the general cinema, but your gorgeous welcome can't quite let me have it. I wouldn't be doing this if it weren't for you. I'm a means of means by no means. I like stuff *from* it from time to time but not having it makes me work, not mad. I ain't got it but I can pay something *on* it. Left to lose, that's just another word for nothing. I'm Frederick the Entertainer, with my tough black ass. I put the owners in parenthesis on my endless tour.

My associations come in long black sentences. That's one of them long, pearline balloons over brush. I'm not gon' be by myself like this with all these people, though, usually, I'm pliant. I won't comply, though I do bend to the hangout. If you force me to think about myself, I'm gon' refuse in my blue balloon. Boy, gimme my blue black cat. Man, I'm going over. That cloudchain you keep trying to put a chain around can't revise this out of what it is. My freedom is a substitute you all up on, sounding like something like clever. I'm not trying to be here, my friend, the first note in the nick of time till its endless run. I guess I'm just not a self-starter, come all this way to be here all by my self with you. It's just like Clairton, or Homestead, in the broken history of Carroll Gardens. It was all just a long history of solitary studio, an

autopoiesis of selflessness like an autopsy of self except the second line couldn't really join in, having aged so constantly. On the other hand, I'm trapped in asking, why am I here? I don't like how it shows up like this, descending into the atmosphere of what I just said. I look that shit off inside as usual, descending into the atmosphere of what you just said, the experiment of critical practice. I said, I don't like assignments. And where all them fucking self-celebratory fucks at? There, in the eddy of my short-term memory, abusing themselves until they cook down low.

These clichés are not but nothing other than my own. Let me borrow some of yours, their tone, their daily speed. On the one hand, I want to hold your hand. On the other hand, I want to hold your other hand. On the other hand, who is this three-handed motherfucker and what is he to you? Who is this bitch, anyway? I'm just playing, Marlena. That little boom of the pitcher against the microphone bears a long history of solitaire. On the other hand, Miles couldn't really play, creaking doors through midnight after midnight with his friend, till his friend was gone, something in the way of sanctified fatigue, something in the science of sound. Freddie taught Miles how to speak in love, though. And now they say that people say, that I found a way, to make you say, that you love me.

This level of intelligent self-consciousness can't seem good if we study for a little while. Identification ain't the same thing as four-handed playing, that long, dry-ass movie, crowded with digital incident in the long history of studio solitude, as if they have to remind you they have to have everything. They *been* impure, and I'm their friend in the air, a range of their disappointments and losses. I want to say they love me a whole bushel and a peck. I'm something loved by them quite violently. In delivering me they push me away so that on stage, my posture is a slight French

twist.

How can self-absorption's cure be more and better self-absorption? How long can I refused to be announced? This would be about my own capacity to
pretend if I didn't have not having. There's no evidence of me, as far as I know, other
than this writing which is, evidently, of so much more than me that I continually
forget my check stubs as I walk across the park. My pardon is denied. Robert Pete
Williams is evidence that this is my computer but "Pardon Denied Again" ain't even
in here, "Just Tippin' In." I'm pretty sure it's mine but I can't find that thing I wrote
about showing up. My kids are in my computer. I took so many pictures of them
when they were little and now I'm pretty sure that's them, and that they're mine,
which is, I'm sure, why I took so many pictures. I'm just playing. But this question of
announcement is connected to the double sense in which I cannot have what's mine,
which I think, maybe, my mama gave me, pinned on me, like a rose, as one last love
song. What I think I am is envoy's last letter. Can you be a message without being
announced? What's the message-effect? To be arrayed in the proclamation without
being proclaimed? Not formally to be made known, but to have been shouted in the

general carolina? I'm not
here but Romare, and in Glasgow,
Baraka,

in the general absence of our nonperformance, deep in the general carolina, shouted "Evidence!" If you want me to play this out for you I don't want to, as if
the dirt of my impossibility made sweeter your impossible air. Do I use the pictures in my computer to secure a personhood I don't want and know I can't
have? I withheld until now, not wanting to announce myself. Now, I guess that's gone. I'm just ordinary up in this, all but not like you. Just like you, all but
almost. Is that just mine or is it shared? That break, I mean. I know you can all but understand me, just like you already knew all that new shit you said. It
was all but we who knew that. It was all of us, almost. If I keep talking about this like this I might say some new shit myself. Because I share your feelings of
anxiety regarding the loss of shit ain't real. I share your distaste for saying the loss don't matter, given that all lives do, especially all the ones that don't. But
it doesn't really matter. Nothing really matters. Everyone looks at everyday shit that way. Ain't no absolute connection between how well you see and how
well you represent. Let's look so hard it all but goes away. Mama cooked herself sick every Christmas, which is adorable, or actionable. Mama,

I just want you to know I still appreciates you.

I'ma write you a long letter and then I'm coming. What I'm
writing myself out of is what I'm
writing right now. I'ma get through with that and then I'ma
write you a long letter. It's the breathing light and I'ma
be their visitation on the highway. I'ma

send it so it can see about you, and see what it means to be announced

         to the general chicago.

             They said, what happened, man? I said, I don't know. Well, we claim that

without proclaiming, sound it out

       to the general inexecutive.

         Please pay attention please, pay attention, son, Zo, you gotta pay attention, man, you never been alone in the studio. You gotta learn how to pay attention, man. Is it something we can share? It's just a story we tell. First it was everything, then it was all, then he said, watching LeBron is just so relaxing. He said he learned how to learn how to be an experiment in the general gunfire. He said he learned how to play the tension. He said he'd show me how we share attention.

    So: 1) Watch the game tomorrow and see what it's like to be able to say that. 2) Say what Zo said he saw in that same amazing grammar.

  3) Always do your homework at school; always do your footwork at home; always shout immersion.

resistances, impromptu

with Tania Bruguera and Fernando Zalamea'n'em

When we reverse engineered the movement, we found the moment it became the movement was the moment we stopped moving. A body politic for newly born political bodies in the drawing of one last breath by one. Pear trees full of rivers all tied up in sugar ditch; pulpit gutbucket molasses still in still, strong and good, but gone. I was born in friction, alabama. I voted for drone chalkline. I died in fraction, california. I remain a posthumous citizen.

So, resist the reduction of non-meaning. Resistance in poetry is how we feel. Grammar striding to divine this weave in not quite seeing. When he says, "to resist is to become a conductive thread," that's what she throws: signal's disruption of itself and code in the common feel. What if we could slice lived experience off the bone? Failure is life, which death achieves so we can five or six mo'gin. There's a black poetics of integrative biology, baby, and it bends like wine. Way too good to be a little bit above what the people say. The people say my mama pinned a rose on me.

We still don't know how many choruses gonsalves gon' take. Give in take is scale off scale: pedagogical riots, transitional institutions, experimental bands. But why does the problem of scale always swerve into the problem of audience? Why does the need for institutions always show up as the problem of scale? Why is showing up always scaling up them lonely streets? What if what the people suffer ain't large absence but small noncommunicabilities? Let's say, with regard to poetry, or music, that small communicability is sound. Then find one and find another one feel good next to it. Put one next to another and sound is beside itself. Line that verge out animal, mantic, anamathematical bruise, subdermal popularity.

Yeah, they are liquidating the national endowment for the arts and scientists need to freak out about that. It's like a breeze holed up in greenblatt's basement. Will the class break up into small, self-taught classes? Spacetime is just an echo of mutual aid. To renew our habits of assembly we need renewable assemblies, like langston's multiverse. Welcome to cuernavaca. Welcome to callahan. Indirectly act to welcome. They can't stop us; they can't even hope to contain us. People in the public better find someplace sufficient for poetry in the market's outer depths. Better make it plain as noplace.

A divan with a double s and a bridge with a blur and a single stanchion. A calatravan bird where bird play jimmy lyons playing bird. A double-fly airborne science opaque in motion, motion all but still, till linda come sing her eyeball off the man. Her method against method is a baby bjorn, gray-blue in a blue-black dive. I can't not get next to you, she says, in rubbed breath, whose expiration politics demands, to which the arts and sciences aspire, as

resistances.

jazz study group, impromptu

with Danny Dawson, Brent Edwards, Krin Gabbard, Farah Griffin, Diedra Harris-Kelly, Yulanda McKenzie-Grant, Robert O'Meally, and Jason Vigneri-Beane'n'em

Michael Veal (v.)
Rebuild, from scratches, from parchment, literally "give a name to" a bunch of times, electronically, as in on beautiful, the corner, from late Old English dubbian "knight by striking with a sword" (11c.), a late word, on vellum, perhaps borrowed from Old French aduber "equip with arms, adorn" (11c.) which is of uncertain origin, but there are phonetic difficulties, embellishments, and lyric hermitage. Meaning "provided with the name of out our name" is from 1590s. Meanwhile daub, the application of paint with sound in poetry, the pinning of roses. Related: Dubbed; dubbing, (off speech with pains taken in Kingston groundings, Lagos) powerdub('d, London Klein bottled), donned, lamin fofana'd.

The lost, desiring floe and glacial building of the book folds Larry Young into something like nothingness. Monk says, "The inside of the tune, the bridge, is the part that makes the outside sound good." He's performing a little palestra so we can study our intervallic activity and feel fly. There's some kinky equations tiled across space in overlaid telling, and swing got tessellated, ruffled and fractured, pressed and stretched, in trade, I mean, trane. Swing in freetime turns poetry grave when you think about gravity that other way, to unsettle the social clock by stacking groove in place. Did you remember the erotic is manual, holding hands with materials that form habitable, persistent, protuberant high densities of soft grind? Housing be grooving fête-massive masceration of the particle, whose traumatic ground-factuality derives, in calculate drift, from evasive, ante- and anti-propositional downslide. Their duress and ours, their violence and ours, unfolding in architecture till, anarchitecturally, we breathe what we share. Grasshopper is free. The joint is jumpin' if the source is open. The definition is a tray of concepts for the spaceshell in freshtime, the hambon'd visiting and carving of its textile, then break that shit in a set of rules we make. If I zoom into the definition, I start to see beautiful ingredients. But we came here to be tortured, our skin alight in gri'd subdivision. Can I walk around it and look at it, see how it curves? Stepping round it drives bursting range out of sounding hollers, open appositionalachia in the labially supple violins of Spenser Dinfiddle's trio x + n. That's the general music of our general circumstance, hiding our subspace flex-material in that brutal, petty world you made on the sea. It sounds good as the subside in our leaves, been leaving, gone. Building structure is a subset of shaping change until the hold, having become fleshly with amputation and embrace, is our ship—a circle with a fold in the middle on the move. Man, ain't nothing free. The joint is jumpin' if the sore is open. It's like we measure it in time, time measuring moving, till we feel the space, place tilling feel, feel her need, her stretch thick deprivation into all them extra meals, sit down around a chain of uneven tables, and underneath the students listen, all in preparation, all out of place in tuning, the circle with the margin in the middle. Man, Joe McFree in fleshdance. Leave the body like a flying lotus, storyboard unbildung. Brent says, "Let's detach the history of the music from the history of the album, its transmedial framing—visual accompaniment, discographical accompaniment—packaged as commodity." Because the music is more + less than that, all not in between every scale off scale, analibrially down and out a long time, like Joe says. "But how can we retain the multimedial affordances?" Brent asks. But how can but not for me not be for me? Is it the transfer of heat, thread to thread by pulsethread, in warm, anorthogonal waves? Fournier analysis roils the water, to keep it simple, as that curatorial thing drones on. Watch 'em remix all that trap onscreen, something like listening to something like gimme some drum in Cuba, some Cubie in New York, while Danny says give the drummer some.

judson church, impromptu

with Ana Janevski and Thomas Lax, and Malik, and K.J. Holmes and Ramsey Ameen, and Clare Croft, and Marina Rosenfeld with Greg Fox and Eli Keszler, and André Lepecki, and Gus Solomons Jr., and Barbara Clausen, and Philip Corner with Iris Brooks, David Demnitz, Daniel Goode, Phoebe Neville and Leyna Marika Papach'n'em

Idiom, which is chordal and cultural, revoices
an irrevocable, irrecoverable throwing off,
some gone off fallenness in pretty falling, the case
of dance off dance if dance is what we translate,
crossing over into falling, throwing off already
given a little bit just in speaking of the language
of dance, even when part of how dancers move
is speech—or what falls, or is thrown, off speech.
Though I'm too unhipped to dance, having a hip
and a half in my walking stick and move, I like to
pirouette like starry night. In my head I be bugging,
sharing jitter in repose, though it's hard to remember
all that company. Adam says it's hard to remember
Steve. We perseverate our severance. We cut each
other off to make each other up. I forget all the time,
so I be going back to church until I'm almost gone,

and Chaski is an Andean message, and the discontinuous
warp and weft of their drumming is our dissolving,
our absolution, our martyrdom before the first martyr,
Cecilia Santiago del Sol, the brother of the beloved.
What if art is the veneration of the brother of the
beloved? She gives before the first one gives, thread
as this ongoing miracle we forget before we forget
the beloved whom you and I desire, not because our
desire is wrong but because our object got to go.
Gone before our object go, our brother disappears
into suspense, a definition you can't override or
underwrite. An exact slur, the true church walks
away in archipelagos of itself, in exodus from Zion
in a dance in which *iglesia* exudes itself in case
y'all want to start getting transitioned. Sisters, flaunt
your new anointing in the street, out past the urban
policy of the park, then come back nude into desire,

in sequined friction, from behind all our surrounding.
The topographical distress of the church is what I'm

trying to put in words. I'm trying to pull this dry rub
out of words into the bare embrace of them beside
themselves beside me. We're beside ourselves together
when she starts singing to abandon all inside. Welcome
all that bowing of her hand disrupting sequence when
beloved gives off beside, *aquele abraço*, all that waving,
that irrevocable greeting, all this raving, irrecoverable
being beside ourselves in common saving, which is not
the same as being, and not the same as not-being, this
more + less than James the greater having gone and given
over in this opening, this greeter who bade me welcome
to that open trio, that rub aubade this afternoon, that great
getting up, that mood for love, or for love (III). Howard
Moody, you come on in, man, you can blow now if you
want to we're through, amen, ameen, all out the box

in being all up on it, in the event of something left to
be desired. Desire always leaves some thing to be desired.
We should leave all that alone. It's the shit sometimes,
but it's residual and we want to be workers in being
desired in walking, in falling across, writing dancing
out of writing without falling, falling in love in dancing
through the church into the mess mass gives away. Is it
the same thing to exude and reside? Is it the same thing
to reside and be left over? Is it the same thing to leave and
be left? Have we left for the lesbian future? Did we leave
for that when we left for church? When we left the church
did we leave all that behind? Fallen for having fallen, having
fallen as all you sexes be too true to be good having been
bade welcome, having fallen for Fred like Ginger never fell,
like Fred for Jill and José haunting, having left holy ghosts
behind to fugue from all up in it, all off, all fallen through,

what else was heavy preparation nonperforming? Marielle's
afformative strike is the general snow at the end of the dead,
let's cool one rumbling, olyakooing, just like the police gon'
come. Now, let's talk about this imperative of welcoming
when the police come. Not when we welcome out of
desire for the shit we have, but the welcome when we
we leave all that behind, the welcome when we never
welcome them again. Why is this openness in saying no
percussive as a beating? Whatever felt good of drumming
is left in bruise. I'm repeating that, having been repeated
by that by Langston Hughes, and in that, in the mess of

Papa don't, Papa don't, Papa don't: Papa don't take no mess,
which is man's elucidation of the law of the father, so you
know all that beauty bears all that beating, all that noise,
then dance to that to prepare to revise in welcoming some
yes, when the image is off in half slash while we wait. While
we wait through the half-projected half-slash of lost dances
waiting for dancers in italics, in the beauty of the general plan
of dancing in the solidus, in this ongoing walking the plan, in
remembering that the police are a pop band, that their greatest
hits all but embarrass the love of Stewart Copeland's time
machine, different in green advent just past Sunday morning
like a bird, the inadvertent freedom of whose non-event, that
nativity again, that here he come like Baby Dodds gets called
by Buddy Bolden, which makes me wanna say callen. Can I say
callen? Will I have to say falled and fail, not start, native again
already, all over everywhere like an inseparable matrix we gotta
separate, I italicized so I can see, and say I saw, from a grid
I gave myself so I could give myself to it, so I could act like
I ain't got nothing to give, which is what we sheave, a slant
we share, a little leaf we leave and mull, some wine we think?

No, the openness of our no is this other no in the seductive
wiles of moving and being moved in rhythm cloth, the beautiful
way my cloth is moved by hand, the caress inside from the one
who whispers in my ear, who seduces falling, courting it in
breathing in my ear now laid to rest, arrested in his breathing
in my ear, the five fingers of his cane inside me to accompany
the story of our injury in the whirlpool of delicious angles, our
inquiry into the general complicity, the subjunctive blow now
if you want to, the prosthetic rest of no fixed point, the rest
of the arrested and displaced, the inured in the secret language
of specific questions, irrevocable, irrecoverable, as if a certain
kind of church that might be where we get ready to leave
church, held in the nativity again of black weather and
obliterate, out of the open in that more earthly engineer.

It lasts through pauses, and continuous projects, in arpeggio
and heft of handing and crosshatched symphonies of gesture.
If you could just feel the weight of your body, it would be ok.
But that's ok, 'cause I can feel it, 'cause your body is my body,
if I could just feel the weight of my body. But would it be ok
if we went out in the street? Let's take all these hand puppets

from the shadows to drift like snow in a broken conference of
who would have been outside to turn the turn away. Eventually,
that woulda been the plan, that woulda been the mood, almost
like being in love with dispossession in advance, what's left of one
last improvising, one last bearing, an unbearably slow climbing
of the stairs and traversal of steam and altered daily and broken
symmetry, and then it's open, too, and then here they come,
native again already again in the sound of all that is the case.

Church refuses virtuosity in fallenness. We fall through virtue,
in virtue of our nastiness, foregiven in giving all we have away
in being given to this sin of turning, promiscuous in spinning out
in all this rubfallen wailing and laughing, all this rubstringed
laughing we be doing all the time, always resisting arrest at rest
at work all the time, in and out of time time and again, taut
all the time, native again already in tuning pans, in preparing
hubkaphones for sharing, step echoed, evening entered, slack
in besidual study of exude. Evangeline, we play our incompleteness.
We disarrange in little groups of little instruments we arrange
all cross the little world we disavow, the one that kills us one
by one. All that's left of church is us in all that beauty, which is
untranslatable if you know the language, if you ain't been falled,
if you ain't been callen, if you ain't been sun and shade by nude.

revision, impromptu

with David Rothenberg, Nicola Hein, George Lewis, Dafna Naphtali, Andrew Drury, Tanya Kalmanovitch, Hans Tammen, Sarah Weaver, David Grubbs, William Cheung and Ally-Jane Grossan

Because we ain't finished with it, logistics sounds like a work song. The bottom anticipates and tills 'til it's time to turn over. Turn over. This limbned, uncoordinated independence is anagnostic. Flesh touches. I am because we are is some bullshit. I ain't because we shair lore and make notes on faith's black presence of an absence. The interval indicates this refusal either to fuse or choose between tearing and binding, a careful preservation of wounding, the whole fade in a shuffle it projects and prepares, a soufflé of angles, a palimpsest of snare and ride, some continually hidden h, a heft of air, a thievish shift carnival, a tufted shear, a shhhh of whirr and bookfan in that we wear a fan of books, page over other kissing inside lip, to disappear into another outside in coming into view. We come from nothing but hard tone row and that cool move, chafing against the new phasis of the history of displacement, sound like it got a three on it to me, black see. Black is the revelation of that which makes a people uncertain, unclear and awry in their action and knowledge. I think I been thinking 'bout that for 'bout thirty years, Krupa become Krupskaya having lost their aura, but when I get a chance I'ma ask Scott La Rock why I start to think and then I sink into the paper like I was ink, like I was a Chinese painter in the hold of Benjamin beholding. The zero degree is what he say he gon' say; she says nothing in reply, a festival, irreparable, Kris in the beautiful corner of my melody, Eric on the side, Ra arranging Cairo, quantum mechanical reproduction giving tune away to rise. Collaborate elaboration, William. Infinite consanguinity, Mumbo. Fleets of drums go with us, bringing something with him, a swing to fold these tortured documents out of solitude. Can improvisation be documented? Has the torture of mothers ever been the sound of burning flesh? Lemme ask Scott when I see him—see if improvisation can be revised. Scott, can improvisation be revised? That's an arctic jazz question, fresh for eighty-eight, regarding whales and, further inland, elephants, and saxophone kids, non-expert users, autodidactic squirrels in task decomposition. What's between improvisation and optimization, bent affirmation and roman ingardenation on improvisational gardening? What's the greek word for reading?

Which is the point of all this rub and cyclone, when the eye falls into plenitude in a series of caressive abuse and kisses, oikopolitics and storms, good and bad time weather in a tore up propagation of clicks. That's when I realized you'd prepared the back of our throat for a speech about the tragic ship, the interminable line to it and the endless line from it, woodskin, wind's skin, wound and drumbone, broth bowed, springboned, time to stay, string, till poise come back for poise, for our unsupported method and post-sculptural stuttering and non-purposive black massive hymn and sold, celebratory subcanadian scotchplain, plummets of bird patterning, sutpen's scotchirish hazarding of north ideas on subhabitually prenational birds, field recordings of syncrudescent birds flew down to tailing in the good and bad time weather, bird in the collective head of mama'n'em at the blues university, Clyde'n'mama'n'em and her and ask and think a digital conference of the birds, viola, 'cause music is the fruit of love and earth and nobody gon' buy it anyway, for there is nothing lost, that may be found in these findings, by these foundlings, driving 'round vising and revisiting in the inescapable history of not being you being all you need. Our name is unnameable in this regard and miles ahead, feeling what you can't see all incompletely. The half-fullness of your glasses makes you wanna make the word go away, but off message there's a capacity for massage that gives me hope, and in the delicate evening software I can understand Russell Westbrook, ulmeric in his unfirewalled all over the placelessness. We gig everywhere and it just makes me wanna giggle, or holler at you from way back then, back here, party over there, if you can wait, we being behind the beat a little bit but right at the beguining, gynomonastically basic and maternal earth tones all out from the tone world, deep in the bass loom, twilight weaving morning in La Jolla/moonlight in Vermont someplace, some folks parking, some just getting dressed, everybody waiting for everybody right now, right there, party over here.

Well moled, old Grubbs! We all here in the ruins but we got something in our hands—an experimental bandcamp for news and flowers. And I appreciate y'all letting me sit in, being so far from virtuosity. I wanna be communicable from way outside. I wanna be in your base community, grace abounding to the chief of sinners. Remember that song by the Spinners called "Sadie?" The one on *Spinners Live!* where he reverted—that contrapulsive, not just knee-deep conversioning he got caught up in? Soul Wynne was sewing that night. It was like he had a drum in his chest, just to let you know that nothing lasts forever. Waka waka waka fucks wakanda up in this regard, improvising forgetting that's redactive flow everyday with all these voices in our coffin'd head of state. These always be herself revising. One said they told us to be Germanic so, with great surprise, we took a picture of your tech with your selves, our constraint, and it was undecidable between us but plantational, since we the police of different voices, to be your instrument in this sovereign fade. Go back and look at it again when we fade a little bit more, when invention won't let us come up on it from behind. I don't know my own stuff well enough to mix it right now, but maybe we be remixing all along, past the everyday fade. Mama'n'em are the different voices in and out your head. You gon' play me now? I wanna play for you. I wanna be played for you. I wanna be down with you. My code voice is Brandy Clarke, some rajautomatic remixive for the people. No way to control it, can't caul it, won't be covered. This that uncoverable cuvée, girl, that prekripkean cupcake, causally unnameable as that Krupa keep coming back, tense but casually, anafricanically curving. Scott says the greek word for reading is writing. It could be, I don't know. I'm undecidable in between us but you can ring my bell. The night is young and full of possibilities, the only trace of which, when I go back, is how I sound for you from one diffusion to another, as if the room were our hijab, as if we were a roomful of Cecily Nicholson writing with Cecil Taylor, as if writing with Cecil were reading James Cone, as if I were Sharon Cone's escort to Cecil's chevronic going home, as if we were the temporary contemporary—air above mountains, buildings in our hands.

impromptu, blanca y bianca

with Isaac Wayne Vancuren, Arti Gollapudi and Bianca Biberaj + Blanca Ulloa'n'em

in a world of trouble, arti cuts the lining of the colored sky. she's lou rawls.

earth shudders, having been reduced to infinity.

the automobile: white on white in white.

solange lays her performance on the surface of white's impurity.

blanca y bianca fold.

a festival of poverty in a brace of sharp embraces.

the most important thing about white, which my mama pinned on me like a rose, is that it is not what it is. that's the most important thing about everything, but it's most important here, since white always be trying to grasp the essence of what is in a fog of graspable essence called what is, which we can see through, though it's less important than our golden circle, which surrounds that fatal cloud with feeling good.

we been swaying on the red corner of 47th and South Parkway, northeast corner, for a long time, and so brutally,

sacred to ourselves in profaning one another, that it's not about infinity, so fuck that illusion, or the illusion of movement, or the general delusion of illusion—just slant groundedness in the grind and layering absorption.

contact theatricality,

in refusing the construction of a false depth, shuns perspective like echo and the bunnymen, isaac's shade over white in the thick and thin and crucial three, shape and bump irregular as loubna lining out the sky's last skies,

anagrammatical,
ante-supreme.
indigenous spray,

whatever you came here for what you came here for is y'all, profane between l and i that i writes over as the pen steps off the surface, having been underwritten by l, having all but fallen altogether all to dance, and preach what you practice,

like barry white.

robert coleman-senghor on the steps of wheeler

with Kim D. Hester Williams'n'em

I would hear I'm so full, I'm so tired. Now, this was carried
as a brilliant smile. Fullness is the river of my friend's smile.
The river is overflown and there can be no portrait. I'm so
full. I'm so tired of this version of the stairway in a hollow
building. There can be no portrait but there is a porch, an
easement, an ease of reception in extremity, of welcome in
having never been welcome. What I would hear in the sight
of my friend was this undertone turned into something we
could share. He was there as what had always been, having
found a way to give himself away through that half solitude
they try to make you try to ask for. What was always there
was that holding of our hands out when the night gets thick.
He would tell us lightly all about that just in passing, smiling,
here, hear, I'm so full, I'm so tired, I'm your patient ancestor.

a common place   flaw

with Octavia Butler'n'em, if they don't mind

The Black Radical Tradition is after capitalism as well as before and during, in multiple modalities always. Octavia Butler's *Xenogenesis* trilogy is all about this, I think, using the scariest life-substance—cancer—to reflect on expansive constantly changing sociality.

Ruth Wilson Gilmore

What's a commonplace book? One of yours is blue. A blue spiral with a little yellow, a little yellow with a sign and a .79. The flaw that would have made me scrape that price tag off is something you don't have. Because your openness to flaw is perfect, you can stay with impurity. We come a long way to love the human taste. You never settle. Walking away from freedom to find a ceremony. Gathering passages of hasn't happened yet in dreaming through what has. Always making the book of the common place.

It's a theme of general application, a salad of many herbs whose scheme is burning in an essay concerning human understanding. The novel is an essay concerning human understanding when you hear the common place. Hume ripped and folded in the open house, home is impossible when you grew some church in broken hume. It's already open so I can't open it. Why pretend interior to access? Why look for secrets when all we need is a margin we can build stuff in and out of? Even if the chromosome is arbitrary there might be true devotion in the fingerprint. Can I caress a thought up in your notebook? Touch a whisper your collective head? Let me make it chroma. You teach me how to want to taste. Got me trading for a gene of the general strike. Your research in seizure is a recess of seed. If we stop, can we grow?

I'm s̶t̶i̶l̶l̶ a child who loves fun and play,
An adolescent—idealistic and unrealistic—
An adult, pragmatic, bitter, and frightened.
Some ash, flung, spent and critical.
Some waving—permanent and gone—
I'm still a feel who loves fun and play.

something quiet, intense, utterly real—even when and where its weird, her f's all curved like e's,

a human wandering, a terraformed Mars, terror-formed, wishing not to be forgotten. *Photocopy all Postcards*. Radio all photography. *Intelligence and compassion* all phonography.

Perhaps there is a "mission school" wherein natives are kept from doing what comes naturally. We naturally make some in some broken skin. We came to read a suit made out of them.

A spider mother submits to being eaten by her young. My kids eat your kids.
This generation I eat you, next generation you eat me

    Fitness determined by who consumes who. Mating is a true struggle with two beings striving to consume one another. They are biologically the same. But when one kills and consumes the other, the consumed one acts as male and fertilizes the reproductive cells of the consumer. We need to grow some flowers through their hearts. *They await the ecstasy of being eaten.*

Flow on flaw is stereo, and I yearn for sisters, 'cause brotherly love is existential theft, an ethics of agriculture when it's way past that, like a truck full of cousins and cushions, or a bathhouse on the run, or a ship in dry rub. But you still hold out a platform for massage in tune. There's so much life and death, and all this generative gone, that you just left a table full of planets, a lot of 'em blue, with stations, and yellow changes. Antigone claims unintelligibility by resisting the imposition of unintelligibility. Lilith broods her brood, her flaw, in anhygienic relay. If you could ever be alone, it would be like every time I say everybody, when I sound the same in assuming every body. But you sound different, and exactly what it is to veer by way of choir, and bend, and liquefy the angle's rectitude. To tweak or twerk or *terkw* or torque like making do. To make *norma* stop and grow like *khôra*.

Your substance is substitution and there's a messed-up warmth beneath stance, an infinitely purple twirl of ground, the enemy within and around in nestle, but it's just some presidents and, as you know, your thing's unpresidented. Raised, urged, ingestion effect; revolutionary gestation; evolutionary indigestion; some blush or bruise or brush or blur; some blue; a little yellow, rhythmed, like the said to never turn that turns the dial. Oh, when I wake up in the morning, the very first thing that I do. I turn on my radio and I listen to Y. O. U.

photopos

with Zoe Leonard'n'em

The question always entails living in the world, but Stockhausen's musical habitat or Dubuffet's plastic habitat do not allow the differences of inside and outside, of public and private, to survive. They identify variation and trajectory, and overtake monadaology with a "nomadology". Music has stayed at home; what has changed now is the organization of the home and its nature.

Gilles Deleuze, *The Fold*

There is nothing inherently unpleasant or nasty about a dissonance: insofar as any chord can be said to be beautiful outside of the context of a specific work of music, some of the most mellifluous are dissonances. They are even to most ears more attractive than consonances, although in one respect less satisfying: they cannot be used to end a piece or even a phrase (except, of course, if one wants to make an unusual effect of something incomplete, broken off in the middle).

It is precisely this effect of ending, this cadential function, that defines a consonance. A dissonance is any musical sound that must be resolved, i.e., followed by a consonance: a consonance is a musical sound that needs no resolution, that can act as the final note, that rounds off a cadence. Which sounds are to be consonances is determined at a given historical moment by the prevailing musical style, and consonances have varied radically according to the musical system developed in each culture... It is not, therefore, the human ear or nervous system that decides what is a dissonance...A dissonance is defined by its role in the musical "language," as it makes possible the movement from tension to resolution which is at the heart of what may be generally called expressivity.

Charles Rosen, *Arnold Schoenberg*

We who are out of sync can't help but be committed to sequence. This promise is constant rupture. The photograph worries us, in this regard, which is shaped by regard and its impossible desires. As images succeed one another, something is supposed to come from them—in the stillness we impose upon them and take away from them—rather than their mobilization. Movement is tainted by stillness and what it's 'posed to distill in us, for us. Does seriality have to align itself with the vulgarity of the timeline, which is held in the sterile fetishization of the singular? Or is there something in or to such vulgarity (an eloquence, an obscure disorder) that one must hold and be held by precisely so that one can't be? These questions won't quite be a bass line, a periodic table of displacement whose preparation is ritually provided by we who get at the bottom of things, where neither the individual nor its opposite can be found. Is seriality antithetical to the pointillistic circularity Mingus'n'em enact or act out or act out of, over the line of music's punctuation? The time of the bass line is spread out, folded, then spread out again, like a realistic sheet. Maybe the contact sheet is music, disquiet offered in every cleft, as crease's trace and foldshade and every shape a cave somewhere, somewhere in a serially whole new shape, mobile punctum moving emptiness through a troubled home, phonic aftershock and anticipatory aural depression keeping airborne repetition underground. But few ever really look at this music. Whoever do become nonlocal, saying, "You see, I am here after all," then saying it again, though always, when they be saying that, here be gone, I gone after it, here and I emergent, after all, in the wake of all's facticity, in pursuit of its subsequent countlessness. What's an image—or a sheet or a show or a page or a pavilion full of images—got to do with the incalculable? What's seriality got to do with all? That's a bend of questions for Zoe Leonard, philosopher of the sequence out of sync.

We get so worried by the gap between what we want from the photograph and what we want from photography that we start to wonder if this phonography, hidden in plain sight's plainsong, is mere ambience. Is the hum in view in the photograph just surround sound? This would be interesting if the background that allows photographic representation to take place were aural. What if it's the sound of the falls? Italics visualize, in *This is where I was*, the mistophonic hush wash over the postcards' liturgy. The tain is some unattainable background noise but, at the same time, a rather less restrictive notion of background might be nice: restrictive not just in the sense of constrained to describe a still obscure mental faculty, but more precisely in the sense of something challenging the very idea of ground, or at least reconfiguring it, because its status as ground is vulnerable to a transformative force emerging from the very "representations" for whom it is a precondition. We want an aural, auratic background that is, as it were, pierced and held, possessed and dispossessed, structured by self-enjoyment and the resistance to self-enjoyment. We want to want a troubled, textured, nasty, nastic, gnostic background; a grooving, mangrovic background with an eccentric edge; a sequential hum that breaks because it's broken, so we can see what the photograph does to the hum as line or plane and hear how it sounds through the sound so we can see so we can see how to sense more fully the flavorful, funky reverberations that emerge from the contrapuntal interplay of multi- and anti-linear audio in the blur and grind. It's not that the analytic of seriality demands the eclipse of any given photo's singularity; it's that analysis of any given photo's singularity is a manifestation of an already given seriality without beginning or end. What if photography—even in the brightest intensities of its righteous and altogether necessary and proper documentary fury—is nothing but the practice of such foregiveness? Photography's continual, contactual post-datedness is made present when the photograph disappears. Photography forbears. It refrains. See? Seriality is dissonant rub; the scrapbook charts a hiding river.

Cheryl Dunye and Zoe Leonard found the meta/physical force of one ain't there—not in the portrait's capacity to give voice but in sounding's revelation of portraiture's essential anarchy. Nowhere in the arkcave, down here neither here nor there, out there all held in exile, our measure the measureless bottom of a measureless fall, we study visiting. Photography takes us in tore-up stride, as the atmosphere thin sculpture shapes with thick inscription—a plain, profane, unworldly coil of accent kneaded on the belly of some water. We walk around it till we find ourselves walking in it after we lose our selves. As an atmosphere for the misplacement of things, photography is an instrument for making findings in loss. Having heard passionate variety of that thickness from all up under home, lifted up over the sfumy phonograph, transmitted in migrant studios, dubbed in mobile study, an instrumental envelope evades monitoring and confounds prediction. Our atmospheric condition is chronic, Miss Carter, but the appositional intensities, knowledge spread out in buffeted intimacy. Woulda been one come after that but can't quite get where we at, after all. Then, underneath the surface we keep scoring, we keep saying all we're left is some pictures.

Image can't quite take place in the world. It might take place through the world, but then it wouldn't quite take place. Take place can't quite get at the apprecision. We hear you talk through image through the world in handing can't quite grasp itself. Can't quite get it but it can let go where come and go displace and skip, barrage, barad, burrage in study. Last night the meeting *gave* place is what I'm trying to say. See? It sounds like an image that restores the earth, which the world destroys. Water falls like a tree's embrace of fencing, which is cared for in a photograph's caress. That tree, which is here after all, ain't quite here no more, or less. Can't quite, let's go.

Wonder if what it is to help somebody along the middle of the way is this quantum strangeness of the photograph? Look how it propels itself, along the path it is, toward the sung, material placelessness it bears. See how she takes us through? This movement, this layer what it is to be moving, which still makes movement through the photograph, sound like what lovers look like: not wind drawn but tore down, tangled up as thorns in number, crying through every rub they crave, somebody saying they did it to themselves. Endlessly in the middle of the way to and from itself, the tree enlarged itself through itself through chainlink, saying to itself, why you rend me, swoon, when limb been gone to meeting?

Art and ethics derive from one another. They drive through one another. Zoe is an anchoress and seamstress. The photograph is divine sewing. Showing is not those shows on the wall. Sometimes we say a show reveals. Showing is modest practice in devotion. Sewing makes a habit of serving. Morning in Alaska, we say, is like mourning in New York and moaning in Philadelphia.

When you're attuned to your attunement to scarring, then you're on your way. A way of walking down the street in Germantown, or the Lower East Side, that corresponds to the making of a trail on the outskirts of Eagle. A way in and out of noplace, for those who thought of making (it) somewhere—local surrealism's frayed locale, unmade in a way of seeing we made, so we could stay there. What seeing? Sewing, inseparably. See, here's the thing photography always shows: that seeing and separation are inseparable. We notice morning is gone, and death shows up like this in Zoe, vis à vid the fracture she reveals in sewing, thereby showing us to sharp inseparability. This comes through sculptural displacement, the swarm and scatter of slow smokelessness, its path-breaking derangements, putting things together that been together, putting one foot in front of the other in that way that walking through burning to shine lets flesh, which cannot be, be serial, which pictures of moving bear, like the uncanny establishment of the fact of free fall really being, surreptitiously, absolute materiality's—or, sociological matter's—flight from being and embodiment, like a river taking bent advantage of the chance to get away from itself for a little while. What if Zoe is the name we give to ζωή, the practice of ethereal waterfalling?

William Corbett calls it "city nature," this fateful, communal differentiation that streets and rivers share. Zoe has faith in that, shows it that way, recognizing, too, that the city and the woods are an arkhive—blood on the vine, blood at the root, abuzz in bloody blossoming, moved in chained removal of trees of swarmy dreams. They work in the wake of the living, too, for whom we care if we care for the dead, sharp as John Keene and keen as Christina Sharpe in the play of redaction and annotation. Retraction spells notation. Refraction notices, undocuments, denotes and detonates and tear shit up and scratch it out—displace the story of displacement with some late, arkcadent abreaction. Is this how blackness works in Zoe Leonard; or how it works through Zoe Leonard in Cheryl Dunye; or how Fae Richards works the long night lounge? Dig in your own displacement and live there. Dive there. Sound that. That's the general principle and the periodic feel of how a photograph, or what is photographed, is neither here nor there, past picturing. O, the baroque and broken foldedness of this black *notando*! Come index edgelessness, spray stain and strain, off, late, ahead, time's serially celebrated (Billie) Holiday, which the bar line's soft, brutal standardization could only stay, and only for a minute. If redaction is anamensural, and anvitruvian as her arm bend, then photography, if we look closely enough at the close looking it requires and allows, is the glisten and quickness that broken surface brings. Deep water runs from stillness, and that's the flight and sound we come upon, moving through it when we move around it, cyclically, pensively, in contour, as social curve.

Earth is dynamic and uncut from its surround, a difference we bear and save in its bearing of our motive dislocation, like a gaitless gait or some Gatemouth Brown, Nate Mackey says.

The exoteric indigeneity of the archive.

We tried so hard to remember what hadn't happened that we started remembering what we were doing right now. Our presence became parietal. Everything folded, creasing, in a kind of common and fugitive wakefulness, the remorselessness of things in their diffusive nothingness, radiant pigment set to flicker. An image of the image is a thing, being held in givenness, in being given away, in being held away in caressive handing. It's like bringing someone, for someone else, neither of whom you've ever met, both of whom you've always known, a mess of greens. Y'all look at one another, through one another, all y'all having been made up by the others for the others, and serially, out of sync and out of round, you say, "You see, I am here after all."

In search of black topographical existence, unheld by the liberal relay between epidemic and cure, care can only hold out for so long in segregation. So, you go northwest to mourn, restore some arc, flown from the world and its pictures back to earth. You find that landscape and cityscape show worked things, things booked in turning, but the move from image to image$_2$ does something else, too, materializing nothing. Diffuse, not defuse, 'cause there's an explosion: the world ends with a buzzplained feel and pictures curl back underground. *Nota nere's* anaredactive force is given in counter-reductive flavor, that low liquor in which film is submerged like words in a bright obscurity of weather that circles out, after you walk around it from side to side, into fuzzy sharpening, edge broad and clean, thrown out and folded, so you can see what she sound like. It's an art of measured chant, calligraphic and post-crepuscular; a solfègic ensemble of value's and the note's soft disarray, past where one can get to, showing where book and score don't quite go together like art and life won't quite come together, either. That's life, where catalogue and show just can't quite work it out. In steadfast dissonance from unison, like a preternatural garden, the distance is some fingertips, clap your hands just a little bit louder. Did Fae Richards ever sing a one-syllable word? Melisma troubles the singularity of the portrait like water. What remains is solicitous ligature. You got to be attuned to the raggedy-ass situation, which ain't about an image of the one who's never there in the first place, or the ones who, in the lonely hour of the last instance, fall apart. One mo'gin let's call this endless wounding sequence. Can there be seriality without one, or (the first) place, or (the last) instance? We ain't from what never comes. We come from nothing that survives. That tilled hard row unslit when you look for the opening come find you, where the image disappears in absent singing of that song called "Scrapbook" that works that new way of folding the never to be naturalized who always be denaturalizing home, as if we were a catastrophic precedent for what we want. Surrounded by it as we look at it sideways, having been invited by it to step aside and dance, it's the *musique concrète* of a photograph you might come upon, almost right now, almost right where you think you are, all but almost here and there, after all. We're held by what's out of this world, out of this world pulled over our eyes, where we can't live. In this regard, Zoe'n'em don't represent one's incapacity for inhabitation; they move as presences in movement sharing endless meetings, placing images and things in question, out of place, in sequence, out of sync.

southern pear trees

Reiteration won't
account for the continuous
exacerbation of shimmer,
elements showing (through)
themselves as other than
themselves, falling in this endless
and beginningless rubbing,
rubbing off, rubbing raw, bruising,
bruising sound,
sound falling off from itself
to bruise itself in sounding,
falling, fallenness in foldedness,
in terrible fruitfulness, in
palimpsestic time, fallen off in
that or let to fall in rising, in
time piercing and terracing,
wasting, embracing, again and
again at a moment's notice gone
violently unnoticed, in the brutal
overlooking of our looking with,
in savage neglect of our caring,
which had to have been shown,
and seen, and sewn, and seen
through, and demonstrated.
Now, here we are in memory of
a miracle of remembering, to
prove the miracle and reprove its
murder, both of which appear in
sustained decay, in living driving
diving in favor of evading diving
into equilibrium, as duncan says
erwin says, as gregg says zoe says
lady says, as zora says janie says,
in sheaves of high-low curacy
and corrosive blossom, of stitch
and echo in caress, of how to
take care of loss and its refusal,
of how to let it hum and fade in
massage like a symphony of open
questions, like a sea dragon in
ashy pear, like a leaning spring,
like an everlasting
invitation to dance that cannot last,
for david.

mess and mass and (

with Harry Dodge'n'em

For Harry Dodge, making work means making a mess in celebration of mass. Therefore, a catechism. Is what it is to take pains separable from what it is to take pain? Is pain absorbed, or reassigned, or can art just take it all the way away? Would that be both a kind of bridge and a kind of break, not-in-between the work and the witness but in their separation's overflow, which the maker joins in the making, having disappeared in curacy, the taking of pain become the taking of care, where taking care in the making, working all the way through the work's unworking, is unbearable pleasure's uncountable continuum? Is the give and take of pleasure and pain what, finally, serially, neither art nor artist nor audience can withstand? There's a dispossessive empathy that makes me stop the world and melt with you. It crushes us, turns our solidities into discharge. Such loss of composure is the work of love that *Works of Love* compose. Consider the pain in the ass of watching paint dry, which is boredom's metaphor of choice. Harry takes on the pain of boredom for the sake of our excitement. But he doesn't really watch paint dry. Rather, in the painstaking shaping of the paint's drying, in the care infused in color's metastasis, in the activation of surface's dimensionality, in the slow cultivation of surfeit, *Harry lets us watch paint dry*, forcing upon us some menacingly chromatic fun because *he makes us watch it melt, too*, our fun cut up with subecstatic fretting. Is the (very idea of the) work worried by this constant going over the edge or is mess messed up in this interminable edging, this continual almost coming that never comes, gone in the perpetual ruination of arrival? Is a mess made, or is this a mess in the making that's been stilled? Even if this ongoing coming done come and gone, it's such a pretty mess (pretty being close enough to beautiful to let the problem of beauty back into play in sublime emulsion, though it's just pretend emulsion, play emulsion, emulsion come again if you feel like giving it to me) that this urethane resin, shaped into active unshapeliness, voluptuously out of shape and unencompassed in the painstaking taking of care and amassing of mess, looks something like the real thing, as Aretha all but says they say and sings in north Detroit with Carolyn and William Robinson and Benjamin Patterson'n'em. Carefully, painstakingly, Harry makes you worry, lining up all these worried, dripping lines all but against the wall, to let you worry the limits of some terms: mess and mass and (care and pain and make and let and line and melt and come and go and work and worry worry worry and paint). It all reminds us, in following color's materiality into the heavy terrain of (something like Jay DeFeo's off-white rose and) Harry's bright confection, that casting pigment is a language problem. The activity of "paint" is all but suppressed in the shift from verb to noun. "Painting" works, or doesn't work, this way as well. "Work" works this way, too, so that art and its terms are just replete with this restless tendency to be still. But if you say that Harry urethanes, or if we call *Pure Shit Hotdog Cake* (which is where I'm looking out from to the rest of this world he works and messes up and cares for) a urethaning, then you might move back into some of that motion. Come mess the noun up, so you can see what's happening. If you'd been inclined to call it a drip sculpture, the movement wants to make you want to say dripping sculpturing, while you go wandering, like Del Gue, the mountain man. Del Gue was a mess, his name even messier than glue in the l having been ifted from it, regifting the g to itself in extra purity. Not no grammar, just messy grammar. Readable as mud or muck or shit, the way a mountain man might read it in being attuned to the natural mess in the name of the preternaturally unnatural. This is the shit and, in this regard, Harry is a doo-doo chaser, doing, working, all up on and after pleasure's irreducible nastiness, its essential messiness, its melting, little mountainous massiveness, like George Clinton and Doug Kearney'n'em. Pure shit is the shit, in this regard, but can messiness be pure or, in order truly to be itself, must messiness fall out of itself and into the all but absolutely fastidious? The careful arrangement of the mess, the painstaking taking care of it, is a deviant sacrament given in the transubstantiation of turds and dicks and hotdogs, or drapes and straps and buckets, and also in the delicate balance with which Harry's shit be all off center on the pedestal, all off center and rough-hewn and strewn all over the room, all thrown all over the place with extreme precision. No divinity shapes these thrown ends, but they do be shaped with burnt profanity. Or maybe this is where divination and profanation converge. Not just to see but to materialize the stinking future in occult practice. Anarranging shit a mile a minute so you can see and walk around in it—talk it, so to speak, with a gaudy, common, spiky swerve. What if the future is just this coming to refuse the difference between what you see and are and walk and talk around in? All caught up in the shit, the thought that emerges is more and less than computation. It's not that information is processed, here, as much as it is that food for thought is digested, cosmic slop cum cosmic birthday party. Cake is a divination engine, not a difference engine, in this regard, though difference is preserved in thick, layered flatness. Walk around (in) it. What is a regard that you can walk around (in) it? You ever wish you could walk around in a painting, which is, as they say, a higher plane of regard? You can walk around in a gallery, but you want it to be flat because you want the tangle even more than you want the air. Or you just want the air to be real close. So close that getting bumped or broken into falls to burning, melting everything that kills us all. We want to celebrate the flagrant crush. We need to take messy care of our shit. Let's sculpt dripping. Let's walk around (through) painting. Let's talk through it till we find the truth, which is the shit, in messi, messi, messi urethaning, installation's literal dimensionality having been rendered immaterial and lionelian in rampant dribbling. The gallery was supposed to be more crowded, so the flatness, which could only be given pictorially, could at least be felt. By flatness, let's mean this absolute proximity, the palimpsestic embrace of the half-closed book, almost popped up in incomplete rub, anabsolute hold. Beholder, see the song called exactly what it is to be close out in the open, to reveal these ana/meta/physical longings we be reveling in past the point of nonbelonging. Divination is a matter of the mother of God, in this regard, and proximity is flow, and flown, having run on through the end, aneschatalogical, scatological, shit! scat! you better get on away from here, which is all you can do when you all caught up in all this shit and all that beauty. Now, can you do it colorfully? Can you make the sausage factory seem like a studio? Can you make all that beauty beautiful and give it away? Harry makes it beautiful and gives it away. He gives away a factory of making so you can make your own groupings and compositions in the room that, then, you make and, then, you give away. You can because you must, angle being everything in this absolute tightness, which is angelic, insolvent imposition. We're you sure you want some? You really want to come in her? It doesn't really matter. You been caught up in the general sculpture, a congenially noncongenital machine, walking around in it as if it were a park or leaking, dripping, from piece to piece, having been both shaped and randomized by careful derangement. You're already making angles and new, one-dimensional sculptures where the pieces, and whomever you come here with or find there, block and pierce one another. It's a hall of complex mirrors and you're not yourself when you look in 'em. And yet you do walk around as if in the deep flatness of a painting. You walk around (in) the curvaceous pictoriality of Harry's drawing, or drying, or directing toward something culminating in assemblage and nonperformative relief, some jamming together of bits and bots and bites into an earthly complication of the world. In this impeccably incontinent terr/afforming, Harry puts some luscious sign on all that melismatic mess that can't nobody tell him how to use. That's why you all messed up now. These are works of love, after all, and messing you up is the work love does. All that making and unmaking that infuses the object falling off and away from itself in degenerative genesis, held among other objects all falling off in beholding one another fall away, all playing mas en masse on the way to mass, being on the way being the mess we in and the mass we celebrate—that's just how we do, all coming all up on where we at and always gone with some tracks to lay. We dodge, but we can't get the hell outta dodge, so we sound like we generally surround dodge main with some general striking, Harry having taken such pains, and such care, that we know what we want to want to want.

fifty little springs

with Aviva'n'em, like we were all alone

the turned origin in leaps and unreliable sources
the way your fold in grace in gutenberg or göttingen
the unset jewels in a fable of broken bread
the beautiful blackness of your kids in moonlight
the way nobody fucks with them out of fear of love

the way you hit me in the eye in the car that time
the way you can't hide even when you want to hide
the way you elegantly sip that warm, woolen sweater
for the hip, upsetting straight edge of your hipcurve
the funny things you do with your leg sometimes

the mutual resistance of arthur's encroachment
the various modes of elliptical pain relief
the archive of archives in your pocketbook
the wind curls tapestries on your corner, too
the echo of it hisses vertically in the music in

the mess you make with a collage of delicacies
the unending way we be all up in your way
the sounding reticence of your publicness
the mirepoix you fuse from my various egos
the black and red valentine as you wander

the new worn trace of analog in your hands
the way you shape their familiar incursions
the way you been waiting for fifty till fifty-one
the way of silt and the way of silk and the way it's
the other way in the breathing density of the lit

in the way you go your ways, pondering their air
the way you share the way you changed my life
the way oh no they can't take that away from me
the way of the book is lonely, now, as you see
the answer is to get us some land somewhere

the need for nine pressure cookers is common
the caramel and burnt ends and thin crispiness
the way miss mattie has become your memory
the up-to-the-minute forecast of your touch
the ray's a desolate condition till it turns

the way our waywardness has gone awry
the way you welcome all our mutant visitors
the way your name brings blur inside
the lost notes we keep folding and taping to
the raised canvas of all that beauty wasting away

the lore of early courtliness that we now relay
the way old friends do to their oldest friends
the actual enactment of intimate gathering
to return to the source for the weapon of theory
the way you pray through exiled pleasures and

the way you wind through cities like a little spring
the way little springs can sing to themselves, relaxing
the way the origin of spring is ritual june,
the turn of original frisk to invisible string,
the insensible, the sensible, and the sprung.

sembalance

with The Otolith Group'n'em

Beginning would have been outside. We tune up on how relation pre-exists itself, sets itself beside and before itself, as resemblance does to semblance as you know, in this sharp curve of calcareous plain you show, sawing and saying what you see and hear through me and you, y'all.

Is balance ours to have, or want? Sembalance.

An asymmetry of sēm, an upsetting of same, for some general flourishing. Such going off together **ain't** quite is or not, which shows up anaphonically, as a matter of hair and stone, sembalance resembling but reassembling imbalance, which dance—that disability—requires. What's the difference between this elegant exudence in our ear that lets us see and our capacity to stylize the derivation of position from position till position is undone, or at least apposed, in hyperkinetic blur? Our critical disposition toward deposition is exudance, in honor of making movement's airy densities, as if white cliffs were migration's residue.

As if Codona were killers of sheep, Stein balancing Burnett in keeping us off stride, falling's ongoing all but falling in the balance of movement making unamerican living in the music out from being and nonbeing, as no one's disorderly history.

The sun is remade in the heat of stones, which is the negative fire of the light table: more and more I hear it when I see it, they say, all the ways there are for people to be resembling in not being one, none and none assembling in the editing of shelter into other swings, a musician not the musician himself, the cineastes not themselves in being else and off, y'all, serving this preservational quality in solemnities of unevenness, in ceremonies of anasimilarity that cinema provides: the fiery preparation of the light table, which is a kind of sliding.

Repeating the whole of them in the hole of each one of them is ensemble, sembalance in consoling eye and ear in touch and slide on mixing, to be resembling and reassembling in nonaligning and lining out in festive blowing, in percussive breathing in aurora, in rapturous corona's flame and rupture, that repeating always coming out in dance's flicker and combatterie of Collin, Don and Nana, and Colin Dayan and Marielle, through Marian and Arazi, with Kodwo and Anjali as anthology through ontology to sample, samizdat, samsara, seam. And seem and seme and Sanskrit. Criticism.

Criticism is empathic scarring.
Black thought is a feather brush of open switchblades.
Show me how to do like you.

our correspondence is an accident

with everybody we don't know'n'em

We correspond in terror. It makes us happy when we hear from you. We try to live by fighting. You try to fight by living. In the dust of your weddings, it makes us happy when we hear from you. Our slogans are baby talk. Someday we'll be together. For now, can you survive, which we can't protect? We look for you in our relative absence. How long have you been in the general presence? Don't you know we're teachers of sadness? When we're good enough to all but disappear we'll let you know. Is solidarity all but this all but disappearance? Then, underneath the show, it's a violent service. Is that the general presence? Our bruise is how we're mesmerized by distance, not knowing who we are or why we fight. The fade into who we are is far away from one another; we're further away from what it is than you. We're this placelessness out of mind and can't quite deal with it. We forget them before you forget that. We forgot, and pleasure and beauty are optional. When there's nothing left to fight I won't have nothing left to give. I'm just like an american; I wouldn't bullshit you for the world. When you see me seeing you will we know what to do?

showing

with Cynthia Oliver, Duane Cyrus, Jonathan Gonzales, Niall Jones, Shamar Watt and Ni'ja Whitson'n'em

Remote, quad crossing loose in four's light movement, limitshade,
blurgrid, touch without looking, frictive footing making music like the people on a horn. Young men, don't drop your sound. The need
of grunt and breath are the making of the music.
Airy hambone, osteoporotic hock, heirloom lattice in an open corner, this mutual
enlargement, this collective amnesty, a riot of rites for giving bodies
away, some miller high life in this funky joint.

Walking hard, irregular runway in slanted circle urging refusal
of joining, she mad, man dem, and it feel like it ought to feel like that all the time, like an old man's inverted saxes,
the impersonality of their impersonation. The sections have proper names—Curtis,
Active Curtis in nonlocal rooms, which is why they kill every last one of us though they can't kill all of us,
ship ahoy, ship of fools, in shambles, like we carrying something. Helen's
beauty is the brow of Egypt, the studious informality of no, thing, face faded in the water it troubles.
We carrying something in the way we carry ourselves down to the waves and wave,
or down to Crossett.

Young men, don't be shy with sound, not give blue lights, look too modern, too
high lift. Give dancehall rupture. Handle the various
proximities. Interview improvisation like Andre, like a sustainable harvest
of apposition, and after you come home from locking, make a salad for Olivia
and spell M
in blackland's cerebral puff. Shakalaka
boom, y'all, which amounts to all this mothering, really,
in audible footprint—a constant signal to the music. Curtis builds, and they walk out of murmurs,
and everybody know: impresovation is the verstimule of the world, running
out of manhood long ago. That's the showing. That's the residue of carrying something more than something
blue.

come on, get it!

with Barbara Browning, Thom Donovan, Malik Gaines, Amy Hollywood, Ethan Philbrick, Ronald Rose-Antoinette and Wikipedia'n'em

21

a war of our own device, a festival of new,

22

documentary consent. The shudder, the
shutter, all that shatter in Bette's eyes
in Jimmy's eyes in Bills' and Barbara's
eyes in all that nothing in repose all but
surrounding all that style we breathe. We
in spiral's handed glance like a rebellious
bird. Like an octave skylark, ajourneying,

23

we give in groups. We been in the music a long time. Can you get that in a poem? Well, if it's in a poem that's just poetry in a tight chemise. A band makes music; the making of the band is poetry: where we stay is a sentence folded in the word you send. How can you make the making of the music sound good? We go to practice in a curve where practice is our theme. Not a game. Sometimes commentary, sometimes inventory, making ain't reducible to its conditions, but it ain't detached from 'em, either. We make cars, the league of black revolutionary workers might say, but really what we're making is the league of black revolutionary workers—all off and under and over the line. What Thom might say is, they thought I was making poems but, really, we were making poetry. We came to keep seeing what we come to in the making. Skill got shared so Thom is them. Thom'n'em, Them downstairs, in a tremendous submachine of milk'n'cookies. To say them is a poet, or a good poet, narrows the scope of the shit in which they involved, a threshold poetry hands when care and study get too deep. Neither the poet nor the poem contains such virtue: it is what it is to be allowed to construct a question, to be allowed being also to be required to construct in an intention—fanned out over the yard like some weighted canopies or a community sing of open corners or a blue conversion of the guards—to hit a poem or a poet in the throat or in the stomach. Man, it's a shame how them fucked up all them damn poets and them damn poems'n'em. And Malik'n'em's problematic of making, in dislocation, is withdrawn, a discourse curved in the outskirts of black performance, left like a broken sequence. "The name of this tune is 'Mississippi Goddamn.' And I mean every word of it," her "and" neither the bending of a note nor the slurring of two but an infinite *n*, endless, endlessly and unbendingly ribboned and turned'n'em, all folded in not in between, unintegered, disintegrate with open gratitude. To think Simone as actor, and Günther as dancer, in Rainer's concern with Benjamin's concern with Bertolt's concern with gesture, genre bent or swirled and neither, is to feel blackness as a deeply energetic position from which to communicate a deeply energetic appositional communicability, all Peaches'n'em all up in all these ongoing epicackalackings to every future meta/physics, wig cocked to the side'n'em, and her'n'em'ean all and every word

of it. You think that all you say of cinema's extravagance of the image is somehow compatible with some fullness of the black subject? What if the movement through the image cuts the very idea of the individual, as well? The specialist wants to stand out from ecstasy; we just be generally going for our thing in little seismographs of sharing tongues that breathe on lips, the social expressivity one can't intend. One can't consent to that. Your genius shows the tangle, the common roots, of the visual and the vidual, but genius is refused in Guelatao. They have ciné, too, but they keep giving it away. They're like a burning shepherd when their

children hold the boom. When
will our children hold the boom
again? What is the vidual? An anti-
sensual seeing in separation and
of it. Then, the visual regulates the
senses, so that that false assumption
is confirmed. Can intoned, haptic
looking give looking back in black
on black enfolding, refusing the
vidual and the visual in goodbye?
Seeing's blind if it can't hear, blur
in blue and of it, unsettled, campy
but unkempt, flaming, shattering
spin inside a curse or curve, cuvée
that animates before the beginning
and after hours, eradicating the
taint of purity from woulda been
outside. Feel that? Funk not only
moves, it can remove, dig? Dive!

The experiment consists of this entangled state being shared between experimenters, each of whom can measure either with respect to   . We see

that if they each measure with respect to   , then they never see the outcome   . If one measures with respect to   and the

other   , they never see the outcome   . However, sometimes they see the outcome   when measuring with respect to   , since this leads us to the paradox: having the outcome   we conclude that if one of the experimenters had measured

with respect to   , the outcome must have been   or   , since   and   are impossible. But then, if they had all measured

with respect to   , by locality the result must have been   , which is also impossible,   and never even gone.

To emancipate oneself from oneself secretly floods the monoinstrumental imperative. The overblown composers guild throws seed, hill by hill, in

maximal scatter. That's liturgical ru(m)ination, anjalalian glossolalia, Jalal al-Din is discourse, well, here we go again. They say you want your freedom,

but all you wanna do is share, deforming life in the terraform, "always a collective differentiation" under firm tara. Somewhere I read you long to
dispossess yourself. What's the relation between emancipation and dispossession? "I'd like there to be space between us and then also a crushing,
a pounding," Ethan says to Eastman, alone, says Eastman, saying "let sonorities ring," which is what King says when he says "let freedom ring," way
past what he means, being eastern man alone. Must we mean what we say? Mo. Meant to say no but mo mo' better in the mo + less than fullness
of its articulation ahh ahhhhoooh after all we been through baby — yeah oooooooooooh we keep coming back to we now ahhhhhooooooh

oooOoooo   ooooooooooooooooooooooooooh   OOooohoooooooooooooo   oooo oo o ooo   Oooooooooooo

OOOo   Oone   out of all   nhhhaah   ooooooohhhh   dawnnnhhhhh

OoooooooooOOoooooooooooooooooooooooooooooooooooooooooooooooooooooooooooooooooooooooooooooooooooooooooooo

oooooooooOOOOooooo   the sweet   hhhaaaaaaaaaaaa OOOoooooooooooooooooooOOOOO   women

ahhhhh ooooohhhhh   oooooooooooo   ooooooooooooooo   oooooooOOOoOooOoOoOoOoo

OOoooooOOOOOOoooooooooo   OOOooooooooooooOoooooooooooOooooOOOOOOOOOOOOOOOOOOooooooooo oooooo   OOOOO   the

world   hOOoOOOOOOOOOOoooooooooooooooooOOOooh   oooooooooohahhhhhoooooOOOOoooooOOoOOooOOoOOooh

ooooh mo mean no + yes, is more + less than no, motherfucker. Eastman, unalone, keep coming back. Is hearing a feeling standing over you like Marx asking questions, Cavell giving sharing as a single affair? Our sharing seems different—either dispossessive of that individuation or held in that all but already given

dispossession, the given giving all of its love away, a haven in never was. And now we got to forgive you, never having gone? Is you ever gon' go? Give it up. Turn it loose. Write'n'em in a state of abandon. Break up into groups and do bad things to *Gruppen*. Is group work done in groups or groups of groups? Is

there anything other than a group? Are there? Or, a little tighter, is there nothing (other than these groups)? Y'all got some more? When is a group too big to be a group? This is the problem of scale. Murray Jackson says Philip Levine's work is work; is work always, and of necessity, group work? What if it's not about putting shit together but how shit fall apart? How shit go <u>together</u> all communicable against the state. This history, in another metaphysics, or none,

art of the fugue, evil nigger, after the difference, out of jail, dead in the street, down on the ground, game in the upper room, through art of the river rouge,

118

group (n.)

1690s, originally an art criticism term, "assemblage of figures or objects forming a harmonious whole in a painting or design," from French groupe "cluster, group" (17c.), from Italian gruppo "group, knot," which probably is, with Spanish grupo, from a Germanic source, from Proto-Germanic *kruppaz "round mass, lump, with an awkward dangling of sticks, a brutal angling of brushes," part of the general group of anaGermanic kr- words with the sense "rounded mass" (such as <u>crop</u> (n.), burr, grained, enherbed,

bitter, pleated with time, like a sheaf of rabe or that rubbed rawness of the general sheaf, or a white mob. Extended to "any assemblage, a number of individuals related in some way" by 1736. Meaning "pop music combo" is from 1958 and numberless, neverones, one, two, bridge. Round ass lump or lumpen from mass in 1967. Lumpen with lumen, or inside lip, a unit of luminous flux trilled in superfluid kisses, from an influenza of switches (such as <u>crew</u> (cri.). a perfect, broken way people be turning to sharply butterfly.

24

dub of the beguine,
is there any beginning,

the beguine then wandering? Orewoct,
the desire that drives one mad, *die minne* to bear *ghebruken*?

Contrafactum, changing worried air
without a change of tune, maintaining
melody when breath is maimed,

expands or contracts, requiring sustenance

in melisma, in double time,

is it too far to think the counterfacticity of King Pleasure and Eddie Jefferson?

Or some kind of scattish
counterfactotem, the sacred utility man,

a one-man band of nothingness, scatman carousing, diffusing, shining in the light that Brent resounds, Hadewijch set to music,
Hedwig made plainchant, Jadwiga jamming, Edwidge Danticanting

a marronage of beguining, running, grounding, praying, singing, dancing in jacmel?

O, how'd the beguine begin, and who all made it there from here? What redirection, what rhum, what rhumba, what rose, antoinette, what Martinique, what
love, what jubilee?   Naw, come on, man! Certain weird, black-ass Dutch women, evidently, and some Burghardts
bogarting for the people—

24.1   Improvisation is how we make no way out of a way. Improvisation is how we make nothing out of something,   24.1.1

120

some ways, that thing, is it the same thing to think and to be? To think and to do? To think and to feel? Let's say that already embedded in this Parmenidean series is the resistance to the very idea, as well as the very regime, of the epistemic even as it's already scarred by it in being held in it, in its placement of thinking at the center of a relation that soon becomes a relational matrix. (And isn't this brutalizing interplay of centrality and relationality, in its very surreptitiousness, part of what decoloniality wanted to be about the business of exposing and disavowing?) This idea that thinking, which is to say the thinker, comes first and everything (else in this expulsive grasp that links and constitutes thing and else in severalty) revolves around it, is a problem of settlement, of the settler who brings the center with him, as him, everywhere he go; now, does the idea→state→activity of "bewilderment" do anything to ameliorate that? The fact that we're still here seems to say that we hope so. But ain't no way if you won't let we. Cole Porter's jubilee begins again and again

and one mo'gin, 1. What if the problem isn't coloniality as an episteme? What if the problem is that coloniality is always already given in the very idea of the episteme? What if coloniality is the age, and the locale, or more precisely, the spacetime, of the episteme? 2. Is bewilderment an expression or a refusal of the epistemic? Is bewilderment in line with other notions—such as *technē* or *doxa*—that seem like they want to want to deviate from the epistemic but all up inside of it, bursting out of it or blooming forth from it just to be curling back up into it, growing out all ingrown so you can't even dance? They put on I can't get next to you but now I can not get next to you since I got a hold of you, real thing, wild thing, sweet thing. Is coloniality the episteme of the episteme, where the constrained motion of from and within indicate a common *terroir*, the general field of scientificity, which is spacetime itself, produced and then discovered? This Foucauldian question isn't meant to advance, against Foucault's grain, an overarching anti-historicism: it is, rather, a question concerning the perhaps inconceivable, but certainly still unconceived, breadth of the very idea of the geographico-historical as such, ravelled and unravelled

in the beguine'n'em one mo'gin, 1, 2. At stake is a general problematic of separation, g, in which case, are we talking, finally, about d'coloniality and b'wilderment as modalities of partition within a spatiotemporal order—a geographico-historical regime given in and as partition? I don't know. I'm b'witched. B'othered. I'm Rodgers and Hart *and* Ella. I'm 1000 1000 deaths, d'. 'Cause this shit? This is me, yo. Right here. Right now. Here. Now. This regard. In this regard, ain't nothing new, Wallace. Just the way I say mine in my appropriate presence. You either need to let all that go or just keep going all up in it without worrying about it or trying to name your way either out of it or innovatively all around it. It's that same shit. Meanwhile, just since I woke up this morning, how many vicious thoughts have I thought about people with whom I agree on 99% of what they say and with whom I share 99% of their desire? Do we want we at all? I guess I fucked up the count. All that beauty. That's bad, and I really want to work on that, I just can't work on it by myself, or in my head, or in the interpersonal diorama, Diotima, Jadwiga, Hedwig, Hadewijch, Edwidge, unsettled edge, upset to music, naw, I see, now, I'ma have to let you go.

25

'Cause what if the difference ain't between art and life?
What if it ain't between performance and practice?

It ain't even between practice and playing.
Maybe it's just all inseparably inside out

and unexternalizable, all and all in
all and more and none and gone,

come on,

anæxplanatory note

ana sound like ani, being not then
        one more time, continually naughty, full in nothing and more, hurtfully
                loving being different
                        in tangled detail.
            like the upper room of bluiett's ebu, like bluets'

unpayable
dues and all around her unpayable steeple, in blue

viewly, ani and ana almost always be ma, mu in a

                mechanics, an ecology, of dispersed mama,

                        she my play mama, my kids'
grammar, my grandma's
daughter, exhausted, ain't quite
            breathe
              right in that heavy water.

    anti

                as the river antes, all that and and yas yas
always

    unfolding, exing, exiting in affirmative
hell naw, in stop killing my auntie,

        my only chance,
        unmissishly dancing offa ann's unmerciful unmerciful me.

        in geeshie and l.v.'s geechie las vegas, that elk's club
wild goose way to stop in and out of step with
            daphne'n'em and that

blew up out of one and two pine bluff duet they in and out of, the dust
        of its explosion that be all up in all our kin, ana,

ani,

steady reciting their sighting, it's so exciting, we so wrong, we gon'
be aiight?
        feel we? fuck the flow.

            the other half of the
                        half that ain't been told
                    can't be told till
                no one tells it
                    nowhere
                            and everywhere
                            to
                                everyone
                        that's
                        all

FRED MOTEN lives in New York and teaches in the Department of Performance Studies at New York University. His other books include *The Feel Trio* and *The Service Porch*, both published by Letter Machine Editions.

LETTER MACHINE EDITIONS

Renee Angle, *WoO*

Cristiana Baik & Andy Fitch, editors, *The Letter Machine Book of Interviews*

Anselm Berrigan, *To Hell With Sleep*

Edmund Berrigan, *Can It!*

Janelle Affiong Effiwatt, *Like a Thin Hustle*

Peter Gizzi, *Ode: Salute to the New York School*

Aaron Kunin, *Grace Period: Notebooks, 1998-2007*

Jessica Laser, *Sergei Kuzmich From All Sides*

Juliana Leslie, *More Radiant Signal*

Mark Levine, *Debt*

Farid Matuk, *This Isa Nice Neighborhood*

Fred Moten, *All that Beauty*

Fred Moten, *The Feel Trio*

Fred Moten, *The Service Porch*

Sawako Nakayasu, *Texture Notes*

Travis Nichols, *Iowa*

Alice Notley, *Benediction*

Andrea Rexilius, *Half of What They Carried Flew Away*

Andrea Rexilius, *New Organism: Essais*

Brandon Shimoda, *Evening Oracle*

Sara Veglahn, *Another Random Heart*

John Yau, *Bijoux in the Dark*

John Yau, *Exhibits*